Human Presence

Human Presence

At the Boundaries of Meaning

STEPHEN A. ERICKSON

ISBN 0-86554-094-2

All books published by Mercer University Press are produced
on acid-free paper that exceeds the minimum standards set by
the National Historical Publications and Records Commission.

Library of Congress Cataloging in Publication Data

Erickson, Stephen A.
    Human presence.

    Includes bibliographical references.
    1. Phenomenological psychology.   2. Personality.
3. Psychiatry—Philosophy.   4. Self.   5. Self-deception.
6. Death—Psychological aspects.   7. Time—Psychological
aspects.   I. Title.
BF204.5.E75   1984   150.19'2   83-24944
ISBN 0-86554-094-2 (alk. paper)

FOR
CHRIS AND ERIKA

Table of Contents

Preface

THIS STUDY IS THE CONTINUATION OF SOME THEMES THAT
I introduced over a decade ago in *Language and Being*. There I stated that

> the meaning of an entity . . . is constituted in part by that entity's
> coming into human presence. To ask the question of meaning, then, is
> to entangle oneself inextricably in the question: What is man? To ask
> what entities mean is to ask their functions within the broad, diversi-
> fied, and subtle contexts of human presence.

What I have not been able to get away from since then is the nagging
sense that human presence is even more fundamental than I had thought
and the disturbing knowledge that I had barely touched upon it. Contrary to much of the philosophical thinking of our time, I feel it is there

to be articulated, but that there is little means currently available for doing so. I continue to find the very notion of presence central to experience and somewhat stupifying. In teaching philosophy in literature classes, for example, I bump against it all too frequently, and neither my students nor I have quite known what to say about it.

All this would have been acceptable, if uncomfortable, had I not come into contact with some psychoanalysts in Los Angeles who confirmed the phenomenon and seemed equally as concerned with it as I. It has been out of this set of circumstances that the decision to publish this book has arisen. I say "decision" because the work falls far short of what I hope eventually is both experienced fully and stated. That it gets said strikes me as far more important than who says it. Thus, at best, my work is transitional, a stepping stone, and whether the stone is stepped over by me or by someone else is hardly the issue.

In the first chapter, "Worlds, Views, and Perspectives," I discuss the worldly and perspectival aspect of our presence to ourselves and to each other. It is through perspectives, views, and most significantly through our worlds—an almost ubiquitous and mysterious component of our language and experience, Heidegger's earlier accounts notwithstanding—that we experience presence. People are sometimes said to live in strange worlds or to live in different worlds. I try to make sense out of this and out of two correlative notions, namely, that we have points of view, and that we gain or sometimes lose perspective.

The second chapter, "Worlds, the Dialectical Model and Death," deals primarily with the extra cognitive features of our worlds. In particular, I introduce a model for construing what I believe to be a fundamental facet of the human condition—self-deception. Our presence to others and to ourselves is diminished through self-deception, and self-deception is intimately related to our fragile capacity to come to terms with our mortality, with the fact that no one gets out of "this world" alive. These issues, self-deception and death, I discuss in relation to some excellent work thought through by Herbert Fingarette.

In the third chapter, "Interpretation and Its Sediments," I discuss the manner in which we deal with our experience cognitively. I offer an account of the interpretive process and delineate ways in which this process can conceal as well as reveal items to us. This delineation is conjoined with an account of two complementary ways of construing the self. Central, however, is interpretation and what I consider some of its very trou-

blesome aspects. *Self*-interpretation reveals us to ourselves. If there is
something fundamentally problematic about interpretation, the very experience of presence, even our own, will be problematic. If the experience
is problematic, a discussion of the philosophical issues involved will be
even more problematic. I wish I had been able to resolve some of these
problems better than I did.

The fourth chapter, "Time and Functions," deals with our experience of time. Our presence to ourselves and to each other is subtlely
modified by our experience of time, and I offer an account of a psychoanalytic and an existential mode of dealing with our experience of time. I
also introduce and discuss a notion I term, timing. Since Kant, time has
been seen as central to experience. If possible, it is even more central to
presence, thus the material of this chapter.

In the final chapter, "Towards Presence," I place my study within the
context of the recent history of philosophy, issue some reminders concerning some philosophical problems that have been ignored in recent
times rather than resolved, and suggest some ways of moving, not just
toward, but within presence.

I believe my work is relevant not just to philosophers, but to psychoanalytic thinkers as well. In particular, psychoanalytic theorists may
find the second, third, and fourth chapters pertinent to the conceptual
dimension of their profession. I should add that philosophers whose orientation is basically historical may wish to read the last chapter first.
Generally, however, I recommend that this study be read from the
beginning.

Concerning methodology, I should make my views clear from the
outset. There are perhaps two major strategies that philosophers employ
in their dealings with their own and other philosophers' arguments and
positions. I shall call the first disputational; the second, conversional.
The disputational method is most clearly exhibited in the work of philosophers who take logic as their paradigm of philosophical perspicacity.
Their main weapons are counter-example, *reductio ad absurdum*, the exhibition of errors in reasoning and inconsistencies in linguistic usage,
and so on. In all cases, positions and arguments are met head on, analyzed, and, hopefully, exposed if faulty. This disputational method does
not require of its adherents that they hold firmly to a position of their
own. What the disputationalists seek to determine is the adequacy of

arguments to sustain positions and the integrity of the arguments themselves.

The conversionalists present a different profile. If the logician is the paradigm for the disputationalist, the empiricist serves this function for the conversionalist. He seeks less to argue against than to argue for— except his "argument for" is less an argument than a presentation, an invitation to view matters in a certain way. The conversionalist says in effect, "I shall be and am presenting you with a way of viewing this or that (set of) item(s). Among my devices are various analyses and arguments. I employ them, however, not so that you might draw conclusions, but in order to foster in you a point of view. If I am able to foster it, your analyses of the (putative) inadequacies of the presentation because of logical flaws will lose their force. Your disquietudes will be no less valid, but they will be felt by you as less deep and less disquieting. My strategy, thus, is to discount your disputational arguments against my position and to resort to the recurring refrain, 'but look at it this way, try to view matters as I see them, and then see whether you still feel prompted to argue as you do.' " It is perhaps an overstatement, but clearly not an egregious one, to say that the conversionalist wants others to view truth, the disputationalist wants others to examine validity.

Clearly, few if any philosophical writings are pure instances of disputational or conversional method. In any philosophical work the two blend, though one method may thoroughly dominate. Generally, disputational reasoning is employed by the rationalist, conversional by the genuine empiricist. More such generalizations are possible, but I shall leave the matter here and plot my own philosophical position in terms of this scheme.

Consider a world—one of the items I discuss in the first chapter and in later discussions of the notion and experience of human presence. A world, I believe, is something a person has, or, perhaps more appropriately, that has a person. Items are viewed in terms of it, and part of the task I have set for myself in this study is to show the means by which the world itself can be viewed. Were my efforts totally successful I would, in fact, engender a view of it, even an experience of it, an explicit, self-transparent one. I construe my task, thus, as essentially empirical and conversional in its methodological dimension. But it is not in fact nor intent a pure specimen of this methodology. Perhaps only in occasional poetry, novels, quasi-representational painting, or drama is this found.

The metaphilosophical aspects of my enterprise, the desire to make contact with philosophers of primarily disputational orientation, and the commitment to preserve unspoken links with philosophical tradition, all serve to establish and enlarge a disputational strain in my work, particularly in the first and last chapters.

There remain a few debts to acknowledge, professional and personal.

I wish to thank the editors of *Man and World*, who have graciously permitted me to use material, now in altered form, that first appeared in their journal in the following articles: "Worlds and World Views," *Man and World*, 2:228-47; "Interpretation and Its Sediments," *Man and World*, 6:9-25; "Views and Perspectives," *Man and World*, 7:103-17; "Time and Functions," *Man and World*, 13:19-38.

Thanks are also due to the editors of *The Review of Metaphysics* for permission to adapt material that first appeared in their journal as "Engagements, Worlds, and Identity," *The Review of Metaphysics*, 27:3-19.

I wish also to thank Pomona College for a grant from its Research Committee that helped make the production of this volume possible. The sabbatical time Pomona College has given me and the warm reception shown my work by Mercer University Press have lightened my burden greatly.

I end this preface on a personal note. There have been a number of people who have stood by me during the life of this work. If they haven't known it, it has been a failure of openness on my part, and if they would think their contribution insignificant, perhaps they underestimate the sustaining power of their personal generosity. All of them deserve mention, but I can only name a few: Dieter and Jo Bruekner, Jerry and Rose Saperstein, Lynn and Nancy Peterson, and John Chen. Finally, there are the Ericksons: Chris and Ellie, Chris and Erika. I owe them more than I can say or than an outsider could reasonably be expected to understand.

I

Worlds,
Views,
and Perspectives

THROUGH MY ANALYSIS OF THREE BASIC NOTIONS—WORLD, view, and perspective—I have come to believe that each is an integral part that is needed to achieve an understanding of human being. I shall refer to human being as human presence. It is toward a perspicuous analysis of this presence that my efforts are ultimately directed.

The boundaries of human presence are experienced as "worldly." It is hard to overestimate the philosophical, not to mention the psychological and anthropological, significance of the term, "world." We encounter it everywhere in our language, not only as it is found in folk sayings and poetry, but ordinary language and philosophical texts frequently employ it, as do scientific and theological treatises. The term is extremely subtle, having a number of closely related, overlapping, and often conflicting meanings. I shall begin my efforts in this chapter with an examination of the term, world, as it functions in various contexts, hoping to sort out some of the meanings of its corresponding concepts. From this task I shall turn to a similar consideration of two closely related terms, "view" and "perspective." Having enriched our understanding of world through an analysis of view and perspective, I shall conclude this chapter with a partial, though unfortunately incomplete, account of the conceptual dimension of human worlds. By so doing, I will have achieved a first articulation of the elusive notion (and experience) of human presence.

Various senses of world are extremely difficult to disentangle. The term is frequently used to refer to a vast conglomerate of items. When it is said, for instance, that the business of science is to explore the world, the term usually means the sum of all items. It becomes roughly equivalent to "universe." Even here, however, there is room for dispute—in fact, considerable room. Does one include irrational numbers on one's list of items? Concepts? Fictional characters? I understand a criterion of ontological commitment is the use of a formula or the outline of a procedure for determining whether a suggested item should be included in one's inventory. The criterion may be very broad and thus quite permissive.

As a limiting concept in this direction, the criterion might allow for the inclusion of any item about which a meaningful statement could be made. If this is the case, one must include on one's list unicorns, Snow White, the square root of minus five, triangularity, the falsehood that Willy Brandt is president of the United States, and any number of other items. Philosophers who take this route, however, are usually careful to make a distinction of sorts between Being and existence, reserving "exists" for those items having spatiotemporal locus or reidentification potential by reference to some one (or group of) spatiotemporal item(s). These philosophers sometime reserve "exists" for that which can be spoken of in a "straightforward mode of speech." However, this notion is itself elusive with respect to content. It becomes easy to lapse back into the view that everything exists, which was the philosophically unrefined starting point. Philosophers such as Sellars, Quine, Meinong, Russell in one of his stages, and Husserl have wrestled with these issues. Their refinements, though differing, are one and all relatively sophisticated. Intentionally or unintentionally, each philosopher delimits criteria of ontological commitment.

Most often, particularly in the twentieth century, criteria of ontological commitment are suggested whose purpose is to enable the world to be identified with the items investigated by the natural sciences. Here, as is most often the case in discussions of criteria of ontological commitment, the criteria do not determine what is allowed on one's list. Rather, a prior decision concerning what is wanted on that list determines what will be accepted as a satisfactory criterion. If one construes *metaphysica generalis* to determine "what is" and a concurrent drafting of an appropriately ordered inventory, metaphysicians take on a strange appearance. They begin to look more like lawyers arguing their cases on the basis of special, predetermined interests rather than explorers of an unknown or conceptually tangled realm. This is particularly true of that branch of metaphysics most specifically under consideration at present, *metaphysica specialis* in its contemporary, cosmological form: the search for a proper account of the nature of the world, construed primarily as the natural world.[1]

---

[1]Even at the level of a predetermined commitment to natural science, matters are not as simple as I have suggested. Consider a piece of muscle tissue. What are its constituents? The biologist, organic chemist, and physicist would list different answers to this question. In the case of the biologist and physicist, the difference would be rather pronounced. Should all of the items put forward by these scientists be included as indispensable to a correct answer? To answer this question in the affirmative would be to deny the ultimate, though not necessarily the short-term, methodological validity of attempts to unify the sciences. A number of philosophers of science suggest that in the long run the subject matters of the various sciences are metaphysically reducible—though, to be sure, not without *conceptual* remainder—to the subject matter of one, all-inclusive science. This science, it is most often suggested, is a terminologically, and thus substantively enriched, quantum mechanics. The subject matter of quantum mechanics thus becomes the object of metaphysics, though that term is carefully deleted from these discussions.

If one denies validity to this program, the result is obvious. In the light of the sophisticated development of a number of conceptually distinct sciences, Eddington's much maligned two tables, the table we see and the table which the scientist "sees," multiply into many tables. The partial success of correspondence rules which link the results of one science to another, translating biological into chemical concepts, for example, suggests, but clearly fails to guarantee, success in the development of a unified physical theory.

Our concern with this matter, however, leads us away from *metaphysica specialis* in its contemporary, cosmological form. In saying that all constituents must be included in an exhaustive inventory of the world itself, we must recognize that the world of the biologist, for instance, differs from that of the physicist. In a minimal sense this entails that the two sciences have different items on their lists. Since the lists differ and the term, "world", has so far been construed to denote the various items on a list, these two respective worlds must be said to differ. If I read the development of the sciences correctly, however, something more significant is meant. It is here that departure is made from the contemporary version of traditional cosmological metaphysics. The term "world" functions in a slightly different way when one speaks of

the world of the biologist

as opposed to

the world itself.

In the former case, world refers not to the totality of items simpliciter, but to items—more likely just a subset of them—construed in a certain alternative way. In other words, world refers to a set of items whose defining characteristics at least are determined *a priori*—that is to say, prior to one's experience of them—by the conceptual apparatus one brings to their interpretation.

Within this second sense of world that I have distinguished, there resides an ambiguity. When one speaks of the world of the biologist, for instance, one can mean either the concepts that the biologist employs or the items with which he concerns himself. These items, of course, are not items simpliciter, but items as they are construed by means of biological concepts. Regardless of which of these two senses is embraced, however, the concept of a world is given transcendental status. If world refers simply to the concepts employed, then the biologist's world is a necessary condition for his experience as a biologist. If world refers to the items with which the biologist deals, then an aspect of his world is transcendental, namely, those concepts which structure that world. Note also the following difference. If world refers to the items with which the biologist concerns himself, we are in the nether realm between two branches of contemporary *metaphysica specialis*: empirically oriented, rational cosmology, and philosophical psychology. If, however, world refers exclusively to the concepts used by the biologist, we have left cosmology altogether, residing exclusively in the domain of philosophical psychology. Our branch of *metaphysica specialis* has been totally changed—unless, of course, philosophical psychology should construe its object materialistically.

In any case, in this second, ambiguous sense of world, worlds are necessary for experience and an analysis of their structures is required if experience is to be illumined philosophically. I shall term worlds in this second sense as conceptual worlds. Conceptual worlds are termed "conceptual" because the concern is primarily in the direction of θεωρια not πραχιο (theory not practice), although this distinction may ultimately be suspect.

Important as conceptual worlds are, they are relatively abstract with respect to the fabric and texture of actual experience. A more concrete sense of world is exhibited in the following ordinary language statements.

He lives in a strange world.

We live in two different worlds.

In their negotiations, they remained worlds apart.

In these statements, world involves a commitment to the notion of conceptual mediation—but it functions transcendentally here, too. In this respect, this use of world is similar to the previous one, but has a subtle and important difference. World no longer refers exclusively to the items construed by means of a particular set of concepts or to those concepts themselves. It refers more obviously to the modes of behavior, the fundamental attitudes, and volitional set—in short, to the *basic posture toward items* which a person or group of people exhibits.

Consider, for instance, the following neo-Freudian scheme which exhibits four different types of worlds in this newly introduced sense. (I make no claim for the scheme's truth as it is used merely for its illustrative value.) The four types I mention are to be taken as overlapping dimensions of normal human presence, and only in excess and weighted heavily in one direction do they become pathological. I limit myself to basic postures toward other people in the first two types; toward change and the placement of items in the last two.

The depressive tends to cling to people. It is important that he be close to them and feel their closeness to him. Yet, at the same time, he harbors a strong desire for independence that is construed as distance from others. The schizoid, on the other hand, tends to put distance between himself and other people. He builds walls of various sorts to protect himself from their presence. It is important that he be protected from them, not, as with the depressive, by them. Yet the schizoid, too, is torn. Even though he suffers deep aversions to people, he craves closeness, warmth, and nearness to them. If the depressive is a clinging man, ill-fit for autonomy, the schizoid is an autonomous man, ill-fit for proximity. He is awkward in the presence of others.

The compulsive desires order, precision, the harmonious and structured fitting together of the various items which fall within his world. He feels it exceedingly desirable that items have a place and remain in their place. Yet such placement tends to inhibit the compulsive's desire for movement and change. In short, his sense of freedom is imperiled. The hysteric, on the other hand, craves movement, novelty, and change. For him, the vital, vibrant, unexpected, and unplacable, because of the elusive tendency, are highly prized. Stability and order are devalued, yet the hysteric admires them and desires their support. If the compulsive is an ordering man, ill-fit for, yet desirous of the freedom of disorder, the hysteric is a disordered and disordering man, ill-fit for, yet in need of stability and structure.

Let me repeat. I mention these four types of world not because of any truth-value I wish to ascribe to them; I mention them in their skeletal form as illustrative of *basic postures toward items*. As basic postures, these four types of world exhibit conceptual structure. Obviously, however, something more is involved. The larger degree of this "more" is what distinguishes them from conceptual worlds.

The experience I shall now describe better evidences a world in this newly introduced and enriched sense. The experience, as the world it partially reveals, is filled with cognitive elements, but it possesses extracognitive dimensions as well. It gives indication of something more than a mere conceptual structure and, I believe, it reveals much about the basic posture of the man whose experience it is. In other words, it reveals a great deal of that man's world, the sort of world which I shall term existential as opposed to conceptual, although it contains an abundance of conceptual elements. What is described is the man's response, put in the first person, to a situation in which he wishes to speak of himself but feels that the other party is not interested in his remarks.

> When the man turns his head away from me and glances out of the window; when he drums his fingers on the desk; when he fidgets with his folders and looks at his watch, I find myself losing contact with what it was I had wanted to tell him concerning myself. My voice becomes ever so slightly higher in pitch. I speak a little faster, and I feel as if I were talking to and for myself—though not completely. I no longer hear distinctly nor comprehend fully what I am saying. I no longer know exactly what it was I wanted to say.
>
> The man is not sympathetic, for that matter not even open to me, so it seems at least, and suddenly—no, perhaps it is gradually—I find that I am closed off from myself. To be sure, I can say what I intended to say if I had thought it out beforehand, but when I say it, I fail to feel its force. It comes out mechanically. I do not grasp the meaning of my own remarks. I experience a disorientation with respect to myself. Neither does what I say seem to belong to me, nor do I seem to relate to it. I find myself alienated, as it were, from the very language in which I express myself. The words I speak are "there" before me, but I do not find myself in these words. Oddly enough, what is said comes as somewhat of a surprise to me. It is as if someone else were speaking. Not that I usually think out what I say before I say it, but what I say usually does not surprise me. There is an element of unreality to my remarks, and in the room the objects I view, particularly the man, waver ever so slightly.

No list of concepts, their interrelations, and the items construed by means of them is adequate to the description of this man's world, adumbrated in his report of this experience. Such a list, nonetheless, would be quite important to that description. It is the extraconceptual dimension, however, which distinguishes an existential from a conceptual world. To talk of a man's existential world is to speak, in part at least, of his life-style, which, to use the considerably misleading language of faculty psychology, contains elements of volition and affect. I say "in part at least" because the existential sense of "world" as I have indicated and cannot overemphasize, includes conceptual elements as well. The extraconceptual dimension of an existential world, however, is what deserves the stress. Some aspects of it are captured particularly well in the following ordinary language statements. Though more examples could be adduced, these should suffice. They are rather paradigmatic.

She felt her world closing in on her.

After they refused his request, his whole world began to crumble.

Imprisoned in her own world, she could extend no sympathy to him.

When a person's world closes in on him, it is not just his knowledge that contracts. His knowledge in fact may not diminish at all. What happens, rather, is that his opportunities for self-motivated, goal-directed action decrease. He finds that he has fewer genuine options. At the limit, his alternatives may diminish to the point where he feels that he has no options at all. In the same manner, when someone's world begins to crumble, it is not primarily his knowledge that loses its cohesiveness. Rather, the person loses his means of supporting himself and giving unity, continuity, and character to his activities. The various reinforcements which encourage his life-style lose their effectiveness. Partial disorientation ensues. The person becomes unsure of himself. He does not know what he should do or how he should be. A person imprisoned in his own world need not lack knowledge of the affairs transpiring around him. What he lacks in most cases is something quite different, namely, the ability to respond to these affairs.

The worlds indicated in these last three statements, thus, have a cognitive deficiency neither as their primary cause nor their primary effect. Clearly, the cognitive structure of these worlds is not what is central to them. Rather, these worlds give indication of a certain paralysis—not, to be sure, without at least some cognitive implications—in the persons whose worlds they are, a paralysis reflected in the worlds themselves.

There is an even more crucial factor involved in the distinction between a conceptual and an existential world. An existential world includes quite centrally a man's basic posture toward himself. *Since a man is to be understood in large measure in terms of his manner of relating to himself, the concept of an existential world, thus, is central to the concept of man.* In another place,[2] I have labeled this truth the doctrine of mediated reflexivity. It requires some explanation and further elaboration.

Among others, the philosophers Sellars and Heidegger have seen it to be of the essence of man that he encounter himself. In the absence of

---

[2]See in this connection my *Language and Being: An Analytic Phenomenology* (New Haven and London, 1970) 133ff.

this encounter, generative of human awareness, latent or manifest, there would be no man. Let me put this point in an anticipatory manner. For man to be man, there must be presence, for, given appropriate conceptual analysis, man is presence. Presence to himself is man's essence. Though not indicated with linguistic perspicuity, presence refers to an act in the broad Aristotelian sense. It is the act of presenting and of being presented. Succinctly, it is an issuing forth as a presence and maintaining itself in this (active) state.

Not only is presence an act. It is, at least, a triadic relation. Note the asymmetry in the relexive relation of presence. In pre*senting* himself to himself, a man is active and projective. In being *pres*ent to himself, he may be passive.

The element of mediation enters philosophically through recognizing that to be aware of oneself is to distinguish oneself from something other than oneself. Over against this other, a man finds and defines— becomes aware of—himself. Initially, this other is that set of items in one's world that a person finds himself confronting.

Concerning the mediation doctrine, two points need be made. First, proof lies less in argument than in phenomenological persuasion. Construe phenomenological persuasion as the carefully worded admonition—one might say, exhortation—to consult experience rather than theory. Experience, carefully observed, should convince all but the most inveterate *a priorists* that awareness of oneself is always an awareness of the singular person in relation to, engaged in, or over against and set apart from something else which is seen as other. But there is a second, more important point concerning mediation. So far, mediation has been given special significance because it is tied to items encountered within the field of awareness. Construe the meaning of within as a less refined synonym for the phrase, "in terms of." If, then, items are encountered within one's field of awareness, they are encountered in terms of this field. This field—one's existential world—has priority over the items encountered within it. Specifically, one's existential world has this priority with respect to the mediation function. It is, in fact, the mediator, par excellence.

This brings me to another important point. The existential sense of "world" involves the notion of one's world being a property of self. A person's world, however, must be construed as a most peculiar property indeed. Rather than being determined by its possessor, for the most part, it determines its possessor, the quality of his life, his affect, how he encounters items—his life-style in its noncognitive as well as its cognitive dimensions. In so doing, entering conceptually into the notion of man, an existential world has a central function with respect to one's status as man—not to mention its significance with respect to ordinary cognition. To repeat—one's existential world mediates one's encounter with oneself.

The existential sense of "world" harbors an ambiguity also. In its existential use, "world" may mean either the items with which a person concerns himself or the basic posture in terms of which these items are experienced. In the former case, of course, what is meant is not items simpliciter—the first sense of world. Rather, one's existential world is comprised of items as revealed and responded to through the medium of one's basic posture towards them. A limiting case of a world in this sense, perhaps, would be one in which there was just one such item. Of this sort of world, ordinary language provides us with an example:

She was his whole world.

To be sure, a world composed of one item is, strictly speaking, impossible. Its impossibility is a conceptual truth entailed by the doctrine of intentionality. This doctrine requires that for there to be an item of concern, there must be someone whose concern that item is, and conversely. "Self"-concern and thus a "self" or "subject" of experience is presupposed by the existence of items of concern other than the "self."[3] On the other hand, "self"-concern is only possible within a context involving a plurality of other items. Thus, if world means the items of one's concern as revealed through that concern, there must be at the very least, and as a limiting concept, two such items. There are always a good many more, as when a man, extending his arms to indicate the objects and activities around him, says,

This is my world from eight to five.

Yet, this sense of world is not altogether coherent. The notion of a world being simply the items of one's concern cannot stand by itself, for its re-

---

[3]I have, and will continue to put, double quotation marks around the terms "self" and "subject" because of their suspect nature. A proper discussion of them is only possible within an extended discussion of presence.

flexive presupposition has not been made transparent. Such a notion makes implicit reference to, including in its concept, the basic posture through the medium of which these items are experienced. When, for instance, one man says of another that

He's always off in another world,

or that

He lives in a most peculiar world,

reference is made to the basic posture of that man, his fundamental stance toward his situation, as well as to the items occupying the man's attention. In short, these remarks refer as much to the way in which items concern the man as to the particular items themselves which are revealed and responded to in this concern.

When one uses "world" existentially, it can also mean a man's basic posture, exclusive of the items revealed by means of it. This use comes into play in remarks such as these:

When I die, my world dies with me.

So, too, at death, the world does not alter, but comes to an end.[4]

One might argue that these uses of world are essentially the same as the ones directly preceding them and, thus, that world in its existential sense is not an ambiguous term. To some extent, this objection is well taken. When I state that my death involves the demise of my world as well, I do not mean to imply that everything that ever concerned me will vanish. Probably nothing will. Yet I do think my way of viewing items to be somewhat unique. If I believe this, I must also think that certain items will never again be experienced quite as I have experienced them. As an example, though it is unlikely that my friends will perish with me, dimensions to them brought out and seen by me may not be brought out or seen again, at least not in the way in which they were revealed to me. Thus, the death of my world involves the death not only of my way of experiencing items, but of some of those items as well—not simpli- citer, but as construed through my experience of them. I cannot help but think this. Further, it is not hard to extend this deeply felt conviction to

---

[4]Ludwig Wittgenstein, *Tractatus Logico-Philosophicus*, tr. by D. F. Pears and B. F. McGuinness (London, 1963) 147 (6.431).

the view that all items experienced by me suffer some impoverishment, however meager, by my demise.

As a final line of defense for this position, consider its commitments with respect to the intersubjective character of conceptual thought. If items are experienced differently by you than by me, it need not follow that our concepts differ. They may, in fact, be exactly the same in structure and number. Our criteria for their application need not differ either. The only difference between us may be in the ways in which these concepts and their criteria are employed. The intersubjective, public character of conceptual thought, thus, is in no way jeopardized by this position.

Having argued against the existence of ambiguity in world's existential employment, I wish now to reassert it—if only for philosophical purposes. I shall use world$_H$ to indicate one's world construed as one's basic posture toward items. It is plausible, I believe, to interpret statements such as

His whole world collapsed.

and

When I die, my world dies with me.

as involving this use of world; plausible enough, in fact to give credence to the view that what I have designated as a world$_H$ has an ordinary language equivalent that refers to it also. Whether it actually and conclusively does, however, is a question I shall not pursue. It suffices for my argument that I stipulate such a use. I shall employ world$_H$ to refer to one component designated by world in its everyday existential employment, namely, the transcendental component. (X is transcendental to Y if X is a necessary condition for Y being the particular way it is.)

Regardless of which of the two senses of existential world one embraces, the notion of an existential world is clearly given the more basic status. If world refers simply to that basic posture exhibited by a man toward items—if it refers, in short, to a world$_H$—then a man's existential world is a necessary condition for his experience as a man. If world refers to the items with which a man has his dealings, then an aspect of his world is transcendental, namely, that basic posture toward items, that world$_H$, that structures his world. Note also the following difference. If world in its existential sense refers to the items with which a man concerns himself, we are in the nether realm between two branches of contemporary *metaphysica specialis*: empirically oriented *geisteswissenschaf-tliche* cosmology, and psychologically enriched philosophical psychology. If, however, the existential sense of world refers exclusively to a man's basic posture toward items, we have left cosmology altogether. We are now exclusively in the domain of a psychologically enriched philosophical psychology. Our branch of *metaphysica specialis* has been totally changed—unless, of course, a psychologically enriched philosophical psychology should construe itself as part and parcel of cultural cosmology. But perhaps the terms "cosmology," "psychology," and "metaphysics" have been extended beyond even a legitimate metaphorical employment in these last remarks.

Heidegger refers to one's world$_H$ as an "in terms of which." This phrase is rather felicitous, if its cognitive overtones are not emphasized to the exclusion of other nuances of meaning. The phrase indicates that in the broadest possible sense it is one's world$_H$ that determines how one experiences items, a doctrine which is preeminently plausible. Whatever problems there are in isolating and classifying world$_H$'s behavior as a linguistic term, experience clearly reveals that to which it points. On a professional level one's world$_H$ is what evangelists try to convert, psychiatrists reorient, and parents and teachers modify and, once modified, reinforce and develop. On a personal level, the problems and promise of a world$_H$ go without saying. On either level cognitive elements are fundamental, but not exclusive. A point I wish to urge in this connection is that the clarification of the structures and dynamics of world$_H$s is one of empirical philosophy's chief tasks. Anthropologists, psychiatrists, and clinical psychologists seek to articulate and, in some cases, to modify the world$_H$s of various individuals and groups. This is, at least, one of the tasks that they take upon themselves.

This concludes our initial discussion of world. Having considered the term, *world*, let us now turn to a consideration of "view" and "perspective." In their conceptual behavior these terms bear close resemblance to "world." Their analysis, thus, will shed further light on the worldly dimension of human presence. Consider first the term, *view*, and some of its variants as they function in the following statements.

He viewed the scene carefully.

His view of democratic procedures was very imperfect.

Her view of his capacities was not very high.

At the time he started across the intersection there were no cars in view.

The view from the east window was quite extensive.

With a view toward settling the matter quickly, he departed.

It was a view of the local fire station.

His view of subatomic particles required him to challenge the results of recent experiments.

In view of his stated objections, they dropped the matter.

The lithographs were to be put on view starting Thursday.

"View" and its variants have a number of overlapping, sometimes complementary, sometimes conflicting, uses. "To view" may mean "to observe or examine" as in the first statement. The emphasis is on discriminate perception. No notion of perspective is introduced into the situation. In the next use of view, however, the notion of perspective is implied, in particular, the notion of intellectual perspective. To say that a man's view of democratic procedures is very imperfect is to suggest a deficiency in his comprehension or understanding. Contained in the notion of view, thus, is reference to intellectual comprehension as something that articulates a perspective on the basis of which items are observed. A view in this sense is closely related to, if not identical with, the cognitive dimension of a world$_H$. Given the doctrine that all awareness and observation is mediated and that such mediation is always, in part, intellectual or cognitive, it follows that a view in the first sense, examination, is always analyzable into the notion of view in the second sense, intellectual perspective. Understanding guides perception. Perception, thus, is always determined in part by one's understanding, one's view. The second sense of view, however, also indicates that not only are observable items fit objects to view, but that items which are not perceivable by sense, such as democratic procedures, are appropriate items also. This is misleading in certain respects. Note that the concept of viewing found in the statement

He viewed the scene carefully.

involves no commitment to the classical, philosophical bifurcation of thought and sense. To view something carefully is to examine and observe it carefully, and this involves bringing various abstract intellectual understandings to bear on the subject matter. To view is to engage in a unitary process in which the cleavage of thought and perception does not hold sway. If one postulates this cleavage, however, the second, intellectual sense of view can be said to be contained necessarily within the first sense. Note also that items viewed can be ordered in accordance with their intellectual/perceptual content. A geometrical theorem, a logical proof, a formal insight are more intellectual in structure than, say, the color red, a symphony's performance, and the odor of cooked vegetables.

When it is said that someone's view of another's capacities is such and such, "it" means estimate or evaluation. This is the third sense of view. It is closely connected with the first two senses, for viewing something, whether sensuous or intellectual, is always selective. Selection is an evaluative notion, regardless of whether it is a matter of conscious control. Thus, when one examines a scene carefully, one always does so with an a priori conception, anonymous or thematic, of what is important to look for and what is not. Also, during an examination, various items are being evaluated as the examination proceeds. Note that certain evaluative elements determine what is viewed in the first place and that, during inspection, the items examined are further evaluated.

A view of something can mean an evaluation of it. Given that this process of evaluation is intertwined with observation and understanding, view can be seen as a complex notion. To view is to observe and/or examine. Such observation and examination involves elements of understanding and evaluation that make observation and examination possible, thus functioning most basically. On a higher level they are also the results of observation and examination. On the basis of observation, for example, a certain understanding can be reached and an assessment made.

That understanding and evaluation are both conditions for and results of cognition is a matter of considerable concern. It might suggest that cognition is circular, that one finds out only what one already knows, that evaluation is simply the explication of prior prejudice. To some extent this may be true, but it is not the force of ascribing to understanding and evaluation their basic significance. Understanding and evaluation make possible an initial cognitive structuring and assessment of a set of circumstances. On this basis, elements in the circumstance are then explicitly correlated, connected, structured, and evaluated. Such activities bring elements previously disparate into new relationships that call for a new, altered understanding as well as new evaluation and reevaluation.

How else could it be? New items come into being as a result of the explicit formation of relationships and establishment of boundaries, but these new items are not reducible to the elements that enter into their constitution—no more so than is the duck/rabbit reducible to the background space and the line which, construed one way pictures a duck, the other shows a rabbit. Let there be no mistake about this issue. Though wholes may be metaphysically reducible to their parts, epistemologically they are not. A man may know A, B, and C separately, but he may also know them as related to form a whole. To put the matter perspicuously, he may interpret them one way or the other, alone or in relation. It does not follow from this, however, that knowledge of A, B, and C, as related to form a whole, is capable of analyzing the knowledge of A, knowledge of B, knowledge of C, and knowledge of their relational possibilities. New knowledge is involved and with new knowledge comes new evaluation and reevaluation. Initial, transcendental understanding, and evaluation, thus, need not be identical with subsequent understandings and evaluations. The difference is often more than a mere difference in degree of explicitness.

The use of view in

At the time he started across the intersection there were no cars in view.

suggests one's view to be the extent, range, or field of one's awareness—in this particular case, one's vision. This field is determined by a number of factors that include but are not limited to: the positioning of the body, possible perceptual obstacles to (obstructions of) the view, and even the understanding of the matter. The first two factors involve reference to the human body and its sensing capacity. These factors suggest the bodily nature of viewing. They suggest that the scope, structure, and nature of one's field of view are determined by bodily factors. The theme that human awareness, construed as viewing, is incarnate has been developed by many philosophers. Later I shall consider this phenomenon in greater detail;[5] here I only mention it in passing. Note, however, that if bodily placement conditions viewing and one's field of view, then the body serves a fundamental function.

One's understanding of various matters sometimes—if not always—determines one's field of view. One's understanding of a given matter de-

---

[5]See in this connection chapter three.

termines that person's access with regard to that matter and the mode of its availability. One's understanding, thus, structures one's view (field of awareness). One's understanding of the political scene, for example, determines which political events and conditions come into view and the manner in which they are perceived. It is not uncommon to say of a man that, given his understanding, his view (field of awareness) was restricted, and he could not relate to a particular event—even though it was an element in the scene, part of the view.

View can, therefore, indicate either the act of observing and/or examining or the specific area encompassed by observation and/or examination. In either case, elements of understanding and evaluation plus bodily positioning and sensing capacities may all serve basic roles. These elements determine both how one observes and what is observed. View most particularly indicates what is or can be observed in the statement

The view from the east window was quite extensive.

Both what what is seen (viewed) and the manner in which it is seen (viewed) can be governed by purposes. It is in this sense that awareness involves and is conditioned by purpose and, thus, agency. (To be an agent or to possess agency is to have purposes, for having purposes is not only a sufficient but a necessary condition of agency. Purposes, on the other hand, are in every case the purposes of an agent.) Consider the statement:

With a view toward settling the matter quickly, he departed.

Here the notion of view is roughly synonymous with notions such as aim or object—something that is looked toward, kept in sight, or kept in mind. I wish to endorse this doctrine. All human action is carried out with a view toward something, with purpose(s) in mind, with (an) end(s) in view. More importantly, human awareness, upon which human action is based, is itself structured in terms of purpose(s). A person with a view toward settling a given matter quickly sees the set of circumstances differently than does a person who has a different purpose or set of purposes. The former person has different types of and dimensions of items included in and excluded from his view than does the latter person. Their differing purposes determine the matter for them. These purposes determine not only what is seen and how it is seen, but determines what is done as well. In this sense, awareness determines agency. Purposive acts arise from and are guided by purpose-oriented awareness. These acts, in turn, modify the field of awareness, thereby having an effect on that field and one's awareness of it. Agency and awareness, thus, mutually determine and presuppose one another. Viewing, in every case, is purposive.

The use of view in

It was a view of the local fire station.

needs but little attention. Here view is roughly equivalent to "pictorial representation." The term, "representation." refers not to the act of representing, but to those means by which the represented is represented. In short, representation refers to the product of the act of representing. This product mediates between the act of representing and the object represented through that act. In aesthetics, this product is referred to as the work of art. (The product need not, of course, be pictorial at all. It might be sculptural or literary. Usually, however, in aesthetic contexts view has its locus within pictorial circumstances.)

A pictorial representation is the product of a selective, and at least partially, representational duplication of a field of vision. This field of vision, of course, is determined by one's point of view—by the manner in which one views the subject matter in question. By representing the subject matter as it is captured by a particular point of view, something is created which may itself, when viewed, engender the very point of view from which it was initially brought into being. If this engendered point of view is then transferred from the product viewed to the world itself, conditions have been satisfied for construing nature as imitating art.

A view need not be primarily perceptual. It may be an intellectual opinion or theoretical doctrine as in:

His view of subatomic particles required him to challenge the results of recent experiments.

A view of this sort may require a man to challenge his own initial perceptions or the perceptions of others and reinterpret them in order to conform them to his intellectual theory. It is also possible that the theory effects the way the man interprets perceptions from the start. Clearly, the old and venerable doctrines of faculty psychology that tend to separate perception from intellection (understanding) are highly suspect. As I have indicated, understanding makes observation (viewing) possible. Viewing must be construed as a unitary process in which the bifurcation of thought and perception does not occur. Such bifurcation is the result of abstraction and subsequent reification. A view, however, may be more perceptual than intellectual or vice versa. One's view of a wheat field can be more perceptual, while one's view of irrational numbers more intellectual. More likely than not, the difference is one of degree, not of kind, and could, therefore, be plotted on a continuum or set of continua.

Consider the statement:

In view of his stated objections, they dropped the matter.

Here, view is roughly equivalent to "in the light of" or "in consideration of." When a set of circumstances is "seen" and judged "in the light of" something, that something functions as an item "in terms of which" those circumstances are seen (viewed) and judged. Such an item takes on special cognitive importance, for other items are construed by reference to it. This notion of an "in terms of which" differs, however, from the notion of a world$_H$, also an "in terms of which." A world$_H$ is not an inner-worldly item among inner-worldly items, but has a different logico-conceptual geography than the inner-worldly items viewed in terms of it. Such is not true in the case of X as it functions in

In view of X, they. . . .

Here the X is an inner-worldly item among inner-worldly items; but it serves the additional function of having other items cognitively related to it and construed in terms of it. Relation to this X is the primary means of determining the cognitive significance and relevance of other inner-worldly items. How, then, is one to understand the relation between an X as in "in view of X, they . . ." and a world$_H$? I shall term the relevant X a view-orienting X. Central to experience in terms of a world$_H$ and its corresponding notion is the experience and notion of orientation. A world$_H$ is never free-floating. It is always someone's world$_H$—more perspicuously perhaps, someone always belongs to a world$_H$. In any case, the relation of belonging to must in this instance be understood to be symmetrical. This someone is bound in certain ways with a world in another sense: world as a set of inner-worldly items. These inner-worldly items, the view-orienting ones that subsequently structure one's world$_H$ and view, so structure them because one's world$_H$ adapts itself to these items for purposes of guidance and orientation. It is in terms of one's world$_H$ that inner-worldly items first come into view. One's world$_H$, thus, is transcendentally instrumental to the location and formation of view-orienting X's. Once located and formed, however, these view-orienting X's exert influence upon the person in terms of whose world$_H$ they are first located and formed. In response to this influence, a person's world$_H$ is subtly modified to conform in its existential and cognitive role to the significance of these view-orienting X's. The way in which view-orienting X's modify and restructure world$_H$'s can be surmised both from ordinary language remarks and through appeal to a simple empirical example.

Consider statements such as the following:

> She had become his whole world—so much so that all of his thoughts came to revolve around her.

> He experienced a transformation. All of his activities were now directed toward winning the competition. Rather suddenly his world had become totally competitive.

> Having seen a genuine art collection for the first time, he found his world stood on its head. It was as if he had become an aesthete. Nothing was experienced in the same manner anymore.

All of these examples indicate an experience in which an inner-worldly function or set of functions bring about an alteration in a person's world$_H$. In the first example, the woman becomes for the man the dominating and, in fact, exclusive view-orienting X. As a result, his world$_H$ changes. It comes to be structured around and in terms of her. In the second example, the desire for victory in a competition becomes the world$_H$ transforming, view-orienting X; in the third, an aesthetic mode of perception. Many other examples could be adduced; experience is replete with them. Instead, however, I shall present a narrative, put in the first person, that captures the experience of encountering a view-orienting X together with its results.

> I was altogether lost. I was off my original path and plunging through the forest. On top of it all I was getting pretty panicky. All of the trees and the underbrush looked the same. None of the familiar landmarks were in sight. At least if they were, I was not recognizing them. As I struggled on, knowing that by nightfall I would be exhausted and without any supplies, I found it increasingly difficult to fight my panic reaction. I stopped in a small clearing to try to get my bearings. But I couldn't. The trees began to swirl around me; I felt dizzy. I couldn't even remember or calculate the direction from which I had entered the clearing. What was I to do? I seemed unable to think straight. I plunged on.

After about an hour—it might have been only ten minutes as I had lost all track of time—I stumbled over a dead log and fell sprawling on to a small pathway. Looking down it, I saw the old mill, and suddenly I knew where I was. Of course, I was on the far side of the old mill pathway. I knew this because I could see the backside of the old mill from where I was standing. Before, I must have been struggling through the dense section of forest between Gordon's lane and the old mill pathway—the section known as Gordon's knot. I was calm now. The panic had left me. It was only an hour's walk from the mill to the village. Having gotten my bearings, I started moving down the path. The familiarity of my surroundings pacified me. I noted by my watch that it was just four-thirty, and I knew I would reach the village by sunset, surely no later.

This example adumbrates a common and easily recognizable experience: the transition from relative chaos to orientation. Because the transition is so marked, the experience stands out. The old mill's pathway and the mill are view-orienting X's "in terms of which," and through reference to, a panicking man and his disintegrating world$_H$ are transformed and restored. The world$_H$ regains structure. Its extracognitive dimensions are ordered, preventing a decline into complete affective and volitional paralysis. The orienting power of two view-orienting X's allows the cognitive structure of his world$_H$ to once again become functional. The man is put straight with himself. No longer is he the victim of disintegration. An extreme example such as this should in itself provide a clear and integrative understanding of the role which view-orienting X's play in the (structuring and) restructuring of world$_H$'s.

There is another side to this account that I have yet to mention. In stating that view-orienting X's serve to *re*structure world$_H$s, I have not given proper emphasis to the role that view-orienting X's play in the initial structuring of world$_H$s. Given that world$_H$s first make view-orienting X's possible, this role is paradoxical. I do not wish so much to *remove* the paradox than to state it explicitly. In a fundamental sense, world$_H$s both make possible and are made possible by view-orienting X's. Each presupposes the other and each serves as a necessary condition for the other.[6]

The last use of "view" I have noted is in the statement:

---

[6]See in this connection my *Language and Being*, 156ff.

The lithographs were to be put on view starting Thursday.

Here view functions as something roughly equivalent to "on exhibition" or "available to be seen." Although it is a distinct use of view, it adds nothing essentially new to the discussion. It follows, then, that view functions in a number of overlapping and complementary ways. So does "perspective," to the analysis of which I now turn. Consider the following statements that are illustrative of its use.

> The details so overwhelmed him that he had no perspective on the major issues.

> His previous experience with them and relative ignorance of the new group colored his perspective.

> Anticipating her early defeat, she lost all perspective on the events of the moment.

> Because of his overwhelming concern for propriety, he failed to see the situation in proper perspective and was, if anything, stilted and unsympathetic.

> He tried valiantly to keep their temporary advantage strictly in perspective.

> When he discovered that only two of them had actually qualified, the whole matter was thrown into a new perspective.

> Given time and a little more experience, his perspective will be altered.

> The perspective which opened for his gaze was breathtaking.

> The perspective illuminated for him was bold. He had never before appreciated the vast number of possibilities quantum mechanics made available.

> He always drew in perspective.

These statements function in complementary, overlapping ways. From them a coherent picture of the function of perspective arises, one which shows the close affinity between perspective and view and their corresponding notions.

The use of perspective in

> The details so overwhelmed him that he had no perspective on the major issues.

is quite fundamental. In this sense to have perspective is to have and to exercise the capacity to see things in their true relations or relative importance. To put something in perspective is not to comprehend it from a particular, partial, and, therefore, misleading or distorting vantage point of view. Rather, perspective functions here in a manner roughly equivalent to "proper perspective." A man who has a perspective of things, who sees things in perspective, sees them in a way that discounts his own point of view to the degree that it may be misleading. The man assigns relative importance to the items and issues at hand, taking his own point of view into account in doing so. In this way he removes such factors as limited vision, myopia, and parochialism from his judgment. Of course, viewing something *in the proper perspective* is an ideal that serves as a limiting concept. One must always deal with issues and items derived from one perspective or another, and viewing something in a manner that discounts the distorting aspects of one's own perspective is a difficult accomplishment indeed.

> His previous experience with them and relative ignorance of the new
> group colored his perspective.

exhibits a slightly different use of perspective. The notion of a "colored" perspective indicates that perspectives can be—in fact they always are—distorted in various ways. In this case, the cause of distortion is past experience. The man's understanding of the past, together with his lack of knowledge of a new factor—the new group—distorts his comprehension. In general, knowledge of the past, insofar as it inculcates cognitive habits that impair the acquisition of knowledge as related to new issues and items, is a cause of distortion. It warps one's perspective. However, the statement can be read in another manner as well. In this instance, perspective can mean assessment or evaluation. Knowledge or belief concerning the past can distort no only one's comprehension of situations, it can also distort one's evaluations. In fact, as was the case with view, it is hard to sort out elements of comprehension from elements of evaluation. The two blend. No evaluation is without elements of comprehension. No comprehension is without elements of evaluation. Thus, to the extent that experience and knowledge of the past influence in a distortive manner one's view of the present and view of the future, it influences one's *evaluation* of the present and future as well. Evaluations, in turn, influence understanding.

Consider now

> Anticipating her early defeat, she lost all perspective on the events of
> the moment.

Here an assessment of an event (supposedly) happening in the future has
a distorting influence on comprehension and evaluation of events transpiring in the present. Note three things in this connection: (1) This
case is parallel with the former case that involved the past. Thus, knowledge or belief concerning the future or past can have a distorting effect
with respect to one's perspective. (2) Again as with view, evaluation and
comprehension are intertwined. Neither can be dealt with in complete
isolation from the other. (3) Having a perspective on something can also
mean "seeing" things in right relation, in terms of their relative importance, as it can also mean intellectual comprehension or explicit evaluation. In short, having perspective—more perspicuously, proper
perspective—indicates in many circumstances having common sense or
balance. This is often an implicit matter and need not have received thematic consideration.

> Because of this overwhelming concern for propriety, he failed to see the sit-
> uation in proper perspective and was, if anything, stilted and
> unsympathetic.

introduces a new factor. Not only does perspective influence understanding and evaluation, but various human concerns influence what one's
perspective is. In turn, this perspective influences behavior. This behavior is determined in part by one's world$_H$, how one experiences items.
In this case a concern for propriety distorts the man's perspective and
this influences his behavior, making it stilted and unsympathetic.
Clearly, knowledge or belief, evaluation, and behavior are ever so closely
intertwined. They have subtle influence on one another. And, as can be
seen, "perspective," "view," and "world$_H$" function in ways that are almost equivalent. At any rate, their functions are hardly separable.[7]

The use of perspective in

---

[7]I refrain from asserting equivalances, for these notions, however overlapping, are not such as to be able to be substituted for each other in all contexts.
The assertion of equivalances tidies up matters, but it does so at the expense of
the actual functioning of the notions involved. Such assertion, thus, must be
avoided.

> He tried valiantly to keep their temporary advantage strictly in
> perspective.

is slightly, though not essentially, different from the preceding example.
Here comprehension of circumstances in the present threatens to distort
the man's view. To keep things *in perspective* is to maintain adequate and
accurate understanding of the various items and patterns of relationships
within these circumstances—specifically with regard to these items' and
relationships' value, importance, and other basic qualities. Comprehension of a present state of affairs, thus, can lead to a distortion of perspective as easily as can knowledge of the past or anticipation of the
future. Also, since comprehension and evaluation are intertwined, it
may be primarily an evaluation of present circumstances that leads to the
distortion in perspective. In any case, the statement presently under consideration, along with the previous statements employing perspective,
indicates that part of the task of maintaining perspective involves balanced comprehension and assessment of past, present, and future situations and probabilities. In many of its uses, perspective does have a
definite temporal overtone to it.

In general, phrases such as "losing perspective," "regaining perspective," and "maintaining perspective" indicate the precarious character of a proper perspective. To have perspective is to be able to
discount, reassess, and compensate for certain (distorting) features of a
situation that result precisely from the partiality of one's perspective. In
its latter use in this last statement, perspective has definite overtones of
the partial and perspectival. In its former use, however, perspective
functions to designate the result of taking these partial and perspectival
factors into account. Perspectival viewing may distort, but one can attain a balanced perspective if, among other things, one makes the necessary adjustments for the various distorting factors.

> When he discovered that only two of them had actually qualified, the
> whole matter was thrown into a new perspective.

gives indication of a common phenomenon. Changes in one's knowledge
or, for that matter, beliefs can alter that person's perspective. A perspective is never free floating. Although it often helps to determine what
one views and how one views it, as well as what is acquired as knowledge
and the extent, knowledge and/or beliefs can themselves cause alterations
of one's perspective. Perspective determines in part one's knowledge and

beliefs, and in turn, one's knowledge and beliefs serve to alter one's perspective. It is a case of reciprocal influence. One direction in which this influence moves, from experience to perspective, is adumbrated in:

> Given time and a little more experience, his perspective will be altered.

Indication of influence in the opposite direction is found in

> Given his perspective, certain facts were bound to come to light and others were unavoidably hidden.

There is a distinct and somewhat odd use of perspective in:

> The perspective which opened for his gaze was breathtaking.

Perspective may now function to designate a particular vantage point: the point from which one is view*ing*. This is the term's primary and most frequent function. However, perspective may also indicate what is laid open to view from a particular vantage point: that which is view*ed*. It is this latter use that is operative in the statement under consideration. Perspective designates what is viewed, given a certain vantage point, which in this example appears to be perceptual. The statement is very general making it hard to tell. A vantage point and that which is "seen" from it may, of course, be mental. This is clearly the case in:

> The perspective illuminated for him was bold. He had never before appreciated the vast number of possibilities quantum mechanics made available.

In this statement, perspective functions to indicate that theoretical situation that is viewed, given a certain theoretical vantage point.

> The final use of perspective I wish to mention is found in:

> He always drew in perspective.

To draw something in perspective is to draw it not as it "actually is"— given an ideal, nonperspectival vantage point. Rather, it is to draw it precisely as one's perspective reveals it. Sometimes one wishes to highlight and emphasize a perspective. This can be accomplished not only by a visual drawing, but a narration, poem, pantomime, or any number of other devices may be equally suitable. The point to be stressed is that the perspectival and, thus, partial and distorting aspect of a perspective, is not always something to be compensated for; in certain instances it is stressed.

The examination of the notions of view and perspective has been a very important undertaking, for it is in the nature of human presence to deal with worldly and inner-worldly items perspectivally and from a point of view. Perspectives and views both enrich and distort human presence's manifestations. For human presence to *view* an item or set of items is for it to observe and/or examine such from a particular vantage point, observational or theoretical. The distinction between observation and theory, of course, is hard to make and certainly not clear cut. Those structures that enter into the constitution of such a vantage point are part and parcel with the cognitive dimension of a world$_H$. View as vantage point and world$_H$ as cognitive "in terms of which," thus, are nearly identical. Complete identification fails only because view has subtle overtones of actual viewing, whereas, world$_H$ is more closely equivalent to the materials, the structures, constitutive of such viewing. On this basis it is relatively easy to see the significance of the motion of a world view. For something to be a world view, the following conditions must be met: (1) acts of actual viewing must be involved; (2) these viewings must (or at least usually) have a relatively common and coherent cognitive structure; and (3) the viewings must singly or collectively range over a very wide variety of worldly and inner-worldly items. To articulate the cognitive structure of a world view is to articulate the content of the second condition, namely, the common and coherent cognitive structure. The extracognitive dimensions of world views are discovered through analysis of certain other features of viewings and views or, alternatively, of world$_H$s. To view an item or set of items, worldly or inner-worldly, is to estimate, assess, and/or evaluate. This selective process, normative in nature, is just the normative dimension of views. It is an indispensable component of world$_H$s as well, and of world views—construed now as world$_H$s "in act." A world view, construed as the active engagement of a world$_H$ in acts of viewing, has what might be termed affective and volitional elements as well.

A world$_H$, of course, is the fundamental dimension of a world when world is understood as the sort of thing indicated in

He lives in a strange world.

In its turn, view may refer to the act of viewing, the nature of the act, or that which is laid open to view, observationally or theoretically.

In its function of indicating an aim or purpose, in the light of which cognition, affection, and action take place, view adumbrates the exceedingly close connection between view-orienting X's and world$_H$s. These latter items can be seen to be mutually constitutive of each other. This mutually constitutive character of views and world$_H$s through the medium of view-orienting X's further ties views and world$_H$s to one another.

The notion of a perspective merges, complements, and meshes with the notions of view and world$_H$ in fundamental ways. In one of its complementary functions, perspective refers to the capacity to view items in their true relations and/or relative importance. In this sense, a "proper" perspective is a view either lacking, or having compensated, for distortions, perceptual or evaluative. The ideal of proper perspective, if applied to world$_H$s, sets for agents the task of correcting world$_H$s so that, when in cognitive use, these world$_H$s better articulate the potentialities and, thus, the functions of worldly and inner-worldly items.

Such notions of perspective and view overlap a great deal as well as complement and add to one another. An analysis of perspective indicates that perspectives, like views, can be distorted—in particular, temporal distortion can take place. In this sense, perspective and view are of a piece. Further, perspectives, as well as views, can be primarily evaluative vantage points, rather than perceptual. However, the statements adduced concerning perspectives add still something more. Perspectives influence a person's understanding and evaluation of items, as well as effect one's behavior through these influences. The same, of course, may be said about views. Finally, perspectives and experiences modify one another. Through various experiences, perspectives are altered and these same perspectives determine in part the form taken by one's experiences.

Having analyzed the intimately overlapping notions of perspective and view, let us return explicitly to that basic notion which they themselves so intimately overlap, namely, world$_H$. What *is* a human world$_H$? I shall reformulate this question, better to pursue it.[8] First, however I have one further observation to make concerning world$_H$s. Though the question is by no means settled, human world$_H$s, I believe, need not be

---

[8]I have carried out this reformulation more completely in *Language and Being*. See p. 162 of that study.

of one piece. A world$_H$, in other words, may resemble language. It may be composed of an incomplete set of overlapping, often conflicting structures that have developed over time, some superceding others, yet being forced to coexist. That a world$_H$ may have a simple and unified structure is quite possible; that it *must* is surely an *a priori* prejudice of philosophers.

What, then, is a human world$_H$? This question, I believe, is the crucial one with respect to comprehending the nature, not only of worlds, but of world views, views, and perspectives. It is the most relevant to unraveling the notion and experience of human presence. The question breaks into a number of closely related questions, some of which will only become clear as this study progresses: What structures constitute a human world$_H$? What are a human world$_H$'s extracognitive dimensions? How do these dimensions relate to the cognitive dimensions of a human world$_H$? How do a human world$_H$'s extracognitive dimensions function in its structure? What is the most perspicuous description of a human world$_H$'s structure? What are the precise conceptual relations that connect a human world$_H$ to the person whose world$_H$ it is? By what means are extraphenomenological questions concerning a human world$_H$—questions that violate the transcendental principle[9]—to be dealt with?

Adequate answers to these questions are so closely tied to the experience of human presence and its disciplined articulation that little can yet be said. Nonetheless, a few provisional and partial answers are possible. Consider what structures constitute a human world$_H$. Clearly, conceptual worlds constitute part of human world$_H$s. These world$_H$s are cognitive and cognition requires the use of concepts. Conceptual frameworks, thus, enter structurally into existential worlds. However, one needs to know what sort of item a concept is, and in what sense is a concept necessarily part of a conceptual framework.

Construe a concept in two ways. In act, it is a rule that serves to guide an interpreting (strictly speaking, of course, there are only interpretings). *An* interpreting is a convenient abstraction. The rule guides

---

[9]The transcendental principle is just this: one can only discuss legitimately that which falls within the bounds of possible experience and which can be made an item for observation—however oblique that observation might be.

an interpreting with regard to the manner in which the interpreting se-
lects items and the context into which it places and connects them.
Thus, were they easily verbalizable, which they are not, a concept might
take the form of the following command: take such-and-such a sort of
item thusly, given circumstances of such-and-such a sort,[10] and place it
in that particular context in which A, B, C . . . N serve as its relevant
partners, enriching and being enriched by it functionally. A concept, of
which this might be an example, is always tied to a purpose, namely, the
enrichment of a context and, simultaneously, of an item by making that
item functional—or allowing it to function—within that context.

Here I must anticipate, in part, what is to come. Since awareness
penultimately and presence, in an ultimate sense, are the summa bona
of human life, a concept always has as part of its purpose the maximi-
zation of human existence. Contextual enrichment cannot but intensify
and increase awareness and, thus, presence. Large elements of the pur-
pose-structure of concepts, however, do not aspire to this goal. They
function much more practically, serving very immediate and mundane
ends.[11] They are indispensable aids in the business of "getting things
done." That they also unavoidably serve such immediate but nonetheless
spiritual ends remains true. I must mention in passing, however, that
the phenomenon of the divided "self," suggested by the dialectical
model, further complicates the picture. More on this idea will follow.

The second way a concept must be construed is as the propensity
purposively to guide interpretation in certain ways when given certain
circumstances. A concept can be construed in this way when it is not

---

[10]"Given circumstances of such-and-such a sort" indicates that man is always in his world$_H$ already, dealing with various items. In this respect, Heidegger is correct in his assertion that man (*Dasein*) must be spoken of in the
present perfect tense *a priori*. Getting behind the limitations of this tense
would be to do speculative philosophy par excellence—what Husserl labels as
"constructivism." It is, of course, hard to avoid this, as Wittgenstein saw in
his attempts to describe how we experience the meaning of a word.

[11]The distinction between *spiritus* and *mundus* is fundamental, though difficult, to sort out.

engaged in its labors but is lying dormant.[12] That a concept is necessarily part of a conceptual framework follows directly from the rule-like nature that concepts possess. Rule is a normative notion. For there to be a rule, there must be a set of rules (standards) in accordance with which that rule is structured, criticized, and assessed, and in the context of which that rule operates. Sets of mutually reinforcing and interlocking rules constitute what I term conceptual frameworks. Such frameworks are constitutive of human world$_H$s as are those individual concepts that enter into the constitution of these frameworks. Specifically, concepts and conceptual frameworks make up the cognitive dimension of human world$_H$s. Mention has also been made, however, of human world$_H$s extracognitive dimensions. To a further consideration of these, I now turn.

---

[12]I avoid the term, disposition, in this connection so as to side-step the Ryle-Geach controversy over dispositional analyses. That I find Geach convincing is irrelevant to this discussion, though may perhaps alleviate the fears of those for whom this controversy and my statements seem dangerously intertwined.

II

Worlds,
the Dialectical Model,
and Death

THE CONCERNS OF THIS CHAPTER ARE CONTINUOUS WITH those of the first, namely, the articulation of the worldly notion (and experience) of human presence. I shall begin with a more extended consideration of the extracognitive dimensions of human world$_H$s. From this task I shall turn to the articulation of a model, the dialectical model I shall call it, for construing human world$_H$s. I shall conclude the chapter with a consideration of death as the clue to understanding the elements of concealment and self-deception that the dialectical model suggests.

To adumbrate the extracognitive dimensions of a world$_H$, I must have recourse to a myth. The logico-technical thrust of contemporary philosophy, much in dominance today, makes such myth-making suspect. I feel it incumbent upon me, therefore, to account for this untimely recourse as a mode of philosophizing.

In the *Republic*, Plato distinguishes the forms, on the one hand, from the Good. As the source of the forms' being and intelligibility, one might argue that the Good is itself beyond both being and intelligibility.

> . . . I want to follow up our analogy still further. You will agree that the sun not only makes the things we see visible, but also brings them into existence and gives them growth and nourishment; yet he is not the same thing as existence. And so with the objects of knowledge: these derive from the Good not only their power of being known, but their very being and reality; and Goodness is not the same thing as being, but even beyond being, surpassing it in dignity and power.[1]

Concerning the Good, one might argue, though Plato himself does not, that a philosopher can at best tell a likely story. Though not true, neither is a likely story false. Rather, it constitutes an oblique and intuitive adumbration of its subject matter. Such articulation cannot be discursive, for its subject matter lies beyond the scope of existing conceptual frameworks. This is not to say that it will always so lie, however.

In this sense of likely story telling, I resort to myth, but I am not committed to Plato's Good. My reason might be said to have something to do with another dimension of Platonic thought—the curious ascription of power to things. Plato speaks of a reality to visible things which is other than form. Things are real insofar as they have power, and this power is itself beyond in the sense of beneath intelligibility. And it, too, if spoken of at all, must be spoken of through the means of myth. This power, closely related to Kant's transcendental imagination, Schopenhauer's will, and Nietzsche's will-to-power, I believe to be part of the ontological furniture of the universe, a part inaccessible to direct, discursive articulation.

I use myth, then, to address that dimension of things which might be termed as their power. Like Plato and Kant, as opposed to Aristotle and Hegel, I believe that power is beyond the intelligibility of form. However, I do not wish to tie my account to the history of philosophy except for fleeting purposes of identification. I am not concerned with the issues involved in Platonic scholarship. Even if what I have ascribed

---

[1]Plato, *Republic*, tr. by F. M. Cornford (New York and London, 1960) 220.

to Plato is inaccurate, it nonetheless serves to identify my reason for turning to myth.

I ask you to construe human world$_H$s as dynamic items, the source of whose dynamism is what I shall term eros. Eros, present as a necessary constituent of any human world$_H$, is the fundamental extracognitive dimension of that world$_H$, its power. As power, eros has two tendencies, sometimes complementary, sometimes disruptive. On the one hand it seeks to be united with, to be absorbed by, its objects. On the other hand it seeks to possess and to make its objects part of itself. I shall call the former tendency the absorptive drive of eros; the latter, its possessive drive.

Any human world$_H$ combines possessive and absorptive elements. When his world$_H$ is in harmony, a person has easy access to items within his world$_H$ and such items have easy access to him. Such a person is both open and responsive and his energy flow is unproblematic. Taken to an extreme, however, excessive reliance on one or the other of the drives can be pathological. Possessiveness can be destructively manipulative, as some philosophers have suggested our technologically oriented society is. Absorptiveness can be suicidally self-extinguishing, as some critics have suggested some drug subcultures and Eastern religions are.

Human world$_H$s have that extracognitive dimension, which I shall refer to as their possessive-absorptive balance. To refer to the degree of human world$_H$'s power, exclusive of this balance, I shall use the phrase "eros-rate."

Assuredly the notions of possessive-absorptive balance and eros-rate may at first seem strange. They do, however, (mythically) adumbrate two central extracognitive dimensions of human world$_H$s and, ultimately, of human presence. Ordinary language does capture these dimensions to some extent, though for the most part metaphorically or obliquely. Consider the following common examples that will serve both to focus these dimensions more clearly as well as provide them with empirical grounding.

> He was so totally absorbed in the activities going on around him that he forgot himself completely.

> She had lost herself in her work.

> The music so moved them that it was as if they had merged and become one with it.

A clutching man, he made everything over into a tool to suit his purpose, people as well as things.

The world only existed for him as a playground for his desires. He dealt with it merely as a means to his satisfaction.

A man of boundless energy, he was able to give himself over completely to whatever he was doing at the time.

She made herself felt as a real presence in the affairs transpiring around her.

As a group, they seem listless, apathetic, without drive. They could neither get themselves into the swing of things nor find a way of making those things relevant to their concerns.

These statements but adumbrate the notions I have introduced. They cannot be taken literally. Undoubtedly and unfortunately their quasimetaphorical content has caused most philosophers to shy away from their analysis. It is not insignificant, however, that our language is replete with expressions such as these and they do articulate a domain of experience left largely uncharted by conceptual cartographers. Through the introduction of the notions of possessive-absorptive balance and eros-rate, I have attempted to make an initial penetration of this domain. Consider now more closely some of the statements just listed.

The first statement,

He was so totally absorbed in the activities going on around him that he forgot himself completely.

suggests the common experience of being taken outside of oneself. Many things can accomplish this and the matter depends to great extent on the person and circumstances involved. Portions of a basketball game, certain aspects of nature, oratory, sculpture, and drama are but a few of the items that occasionally serve this function. Some mystical religious experiences as well are described in a way that indicate their strong family resemblance to these more common phenomena. In any case, to be taken outside of oneself is to be "self-forgetfully" absorbed in something. If by "self" is meant in part the (asymmetrically) reflexive relation of self-*awareness*, then such self-forgetful absorption engenders selflessness. Surely this is a common experience. Rather than explicating it by means of an empirically based theory of personality, I merely introduce the pre-personal notion of absorptive drive. This notion is meant to catch the common, usually fleeting, though sometimes intense and enduring, experience of being caught up in something.

A person can be engrossed in something to a degree that it seems to determine him, rather than he it. To use current and common terminology, a person in this circumstance is totally and nonmanipulatively involved. He is *into* and *subject to* whatever so involves him. He experiences the object of his involvement as determining him. He responds and reacts to its demands. Sometimes the object is experienced as so worthy that it is altogether natural for a person to give himself over to it. This is clearly part of the dogmatic structure of religious doctrine, though, unfortunately, not always a part of religious experience.

Perhaps for the present age, experiences of infatuation and love provide a more universal ground for explicating that which I indicate with the phrase "absorptive drive." In these experiences the value judgment of worthiness does not so much attach to the object—be it the loved one or the love relationship. Rather, during those inevitable times when reflection takes place, one finds the object to be fulfilling, meaningful. It calls for a loyalty that puts one at its service. This is because the object is experienced as consuming and absorbing. Religiously inclined people sometime term it "saving."

Clearly there are methodological difficulties involved in any attempt to adumbrate that extracognitive dimension of a world$_H$ termed "absorptive drive." More often than not, the experience to which the phrase refers is explicated through appeal to religious or abnormal psychological phenomena. Such phenomena do exhibit the characteristics in need of display. But to base one's appeal on these phenomena is tactically wrong. Critics of these positions as well as expounders tend to tie the experiences themselves to religious commitments or theories of personality. Because these critics wish to deny the truth of religious statements or the ultimate philosophical feasibility of certain theories of personality, they find themselves denying the phenomena out of which the religious and/or psychological doctrines arise.

Here, certainly, the critics go wrong. My claim with regard to these reputed religious and/or abnormally psychological experiences is twofold: (1) that these experiences differ only in degree from common, everyday experiences; and (2) that one can accept, as one must *qua* phenomenologist, the experiences themselves while suspending judgment and perhaps ultimately denying their psychological and/or religious

interpretation. To avoid terribly misleading controversies, I have delib-
erately chosen very common examples to illustrate absorptive drive. I
have used similar, everyday examples to illustrate possessive drive and
eros-rate as well. I wish to introduce neither a religious nor a psychological theory to explain these phenomena.

The notions I introduce are pre-personal and, with regard to psychology and religion, neutral and non-commital. This last statement,
however, raises some issues. To be sure, description—pure, unadulter-
ated, and totally devoid of explanatory factors—is impossible. This pro-
grammatic criticism of the phenomenological enterprise is thoroughly
justified. Unfortunately, the criticism fails to take into account the
equally important truth that the explanation/description ratio is expli-
cable in terms of degrees. In introducing the notions of possessive drive,
absorptive drive, and eros-rate, it is possible to limit severely the explanatory content. This I have done. Explanation and description must
never be construed as operating together in accordance with the logical
law of exclusive alternation. This would make no empirical sense. The
important strategy for the phenomenologist to follow is to reduce the explanatory factor. He need not pursue the illusory ideal of eliminating
this factor altogether.

The second statement illustrating absorptive drive,

She had lost herself in her work.

differs only in small measure from the first. Sometimes the activity of
doing something lifts a person out of a state either of lethargy or of possessiveness. Sometimes, however, work is a possessive act. Concerning
this possibility, an explanation is in order.

Freud is not wrong in suggesting work (labor) as one way, along with
love, of working out one's salvation. The cure for the narcissistic neuroses and for narcissism in general has as its result getting outside of oneself and becoming absorbed in surrounding things. Marx's notion of a
non-alienated form of labor—the free, self-realizing, existential activity
of human beings—supposedly has the same result. Marx, of course,
casts the result in socio-economic terms, not primarily in psychological
ones. In either case, however, construe work as the act of giving oneself
over to the demands—perhaps one should say, the lure—of a subject
matter and letting it determine what one does and how one does it. Pro-
ceed by construing the work as absorbing, so absorbing that one is in its

service, fulfilled and made self-forgetfully carefree by it. To be sure, this is just one way in which work can be engaged. In this form, the concept of work is very closely related to Schiller's notion of play. Nietzsche has something of this sort in mind when he writes,

Man's maturity: To have regained the seriousness that he had as a child at play.[2]

Work can, however, take on a different character. One can mold, warp, and distort the subject matter to one's own demands. Because the work is "consciously" and calculatingly undertaken, a person's own self-conscious ends determine what is done and how one goes about it. Work of this sort does not *absorb* a person, rather, it is manipulatively ruled and incorporated into that person's purposes. Use transforms into *ab*use. Work becomes the self-conscious appropriation of something to one's own demands. Such work must be construed as possessive. Existential philosophers and cultural and ecological prophets often accuse modern technology of being of this—being of an essentially destructive nature. Technological work, it is said, violates the integrity of the objects with which it deals.

The absorptive and the possessive, then, are two categorically distinct ways of demarcating forms of labor conceptually. Though the two virtually always appear in mixed form, combined in various ways with each other, they are conceptually distinct. (Of course, there are other categories of labor; compulsive, repetitive, and mechanical are just a few.)

The statement,

The music so moved them, that it was as if they had merged and become one with it.

indicates an absorptive power possessed by an aesthetic phenomenon. More perspicuously construed, the statement indicates the power of a particular aesthetic item to elicit human presence's absorptive drive. Clearly any phenomenon, under appropriate circumstances, can possess this power. Traditionally, however, aesthetic phenomena have been credited with this capacity. Schopenhauer indicates the fleeting, absorption-eliciting power of the aesthetic in his remarks concerning deliverance

---

[2]Nietzsche, *Beyond Good and Evil*, tr. by Marianne Cowan (Chicago, 1959) 77.

from the dominance of the will. Given appropriate qualifications, Nietzsche, too, has something of this sort in mind in *The Birth of Tragedy* and in his later remarks concerning art. Though any item may conceivably have the power to elicit absorptive drive, religious and aesthetic items and circumstances have traditionally been singled out as prime possessors of this capacity.

Consider now the statement,

> A clutching man, he made everything over into a tool to suit his purposes, people as well as things.

Here a situation of a possessive sort is encountered. Possess takes the form of transforming inner-worldly items into items to be used for human presence's various purposes. A tool is, for all intents and purposes, an extension of its user, and as an extension and under its user's control, the tool can be viewed as part of the user. As a tool, the inner-worldly item gets incorporated into the user's sphere of activity.

The important factor to note in this situation, as well as in the situation adumbrated in

> The world only existed for him as a playground for his desires. He dealt with it merely as a means to his satisfaction.

is that the integrity of inner-worldly items is violated. Rather than being viewed as items with a life of their own, having potentialities in whose service human presence stand, the items are construed merely in terms of their potential with regard to the satisfaction of specific human desires. In this way their comprehension is warped, their reality distorted, and their possible range of activity constricted. When an item is viewed simply in terms of its possible human use, an *ab*use is involved. Such abuse, some critics claim, is integral to the development of a technological society. Without passing judgment on this allegation, it can clearly be seen that the world of the compulsive has this abusive quality to it.

It must be said that use is not always abuse. Do not think that any and every use of an item constitutes its abuse or a possessive misappropriation of it. This would be far too simplified. Construe items as having a number of potentialities. Because they stand in relation to human presence, these potentialities get articulated in varying degrees. Some potentialities have to do with specific human purposes, while others require that human presence stand in the service of the inner-worldly items whose potentialities they are. The interaction between human presence and inner-worldly items is a subtle affair. If the usefulness of inner-worldly items becomes the overwhelmingly dominant concern, however, there has been a possessive perversion of these items. The cause is the possessive/absorptive imbalance (and thus perversion) of that human presence which so relates to them. The imbalance, of course, is on the possessive side. Technology, capitalism, and compulsive-obsessive neuroses have all been construed in one way or another as possessive pathologies by various critics of life and culture. On the other hand, an imbalance on the absorptive side can be equally pathological. Inner-worldly items not only have potentialities of their own, in whose service human presence stands—metaphorical as this notion must obviously sound—but these items' potentialities also attain a certain measure of functional status through that usefulness of theirs that arises from interaction with human presence. As I said, use is not always abuse. It is sometimes the pragmatico-cognitive fruition both of inner-worldly items and human presence. Possessive and absorptive drives must attain and maintain a balance if human presence and the inner-worldly items with which it interacts are to have genuine autonomy and integrity.

Eros-rate is still another consideration. The first statement is specifically illustrative of this phenomenon:

> A man of boundless energy, he was able to give himself over completely
> to whatever he was doing at the time.

Generally speaking, the intensification of either possessive/absorptive drive requires the expenditure of energy, and to speak of eros-rate is to have in mind something closely akin to energy level or the degree of power or amount of strength possessed by an agent. Clearly, a person with a high energy level or, alternatively, considerable power or strength of agency is able to get outside of himself and into active contact with more inner-worldly items within his world$_H$ far easier than the person with a low eros-rate. Engaging in an activity, whether it be mental or physical, demands a certain outlay of energy and the person whose eros-rate is high has more expendable energy than does the person whose rate is low.

The notion of eros-rate is meant to capture the concept of degrees of available energy. Note two points in passing. First, energy expenditure needs by no means to result in its irrevocable loss. Rather, through the use of power, more power is gained. Anyone who has worked hard, expending a great deal of energy, knows the truth of this—regardless of whether his work was mental or physical. The buildup of strength, psychic or physical, comes through its use. This was one of Nietzsche's many insights concerning the will-to-power. Second, the notion of a degree of power or an amount of strength possessed by an agent has to do with what might be termed the strength or power of agency itself. This notion cuts across the distinction between mental and physical. In short, it undercuts this latter distinction.

The statement,

> She made herself felt as a real presence in the affairs transpiring around her.

is immensely important. It adumbrates empirically that human presence is as much a matter of energy as it is a cognitive notion. Too often human presence gets construed merely as one of the cognitive termini in the knower/known relation. Cognition is taken to be a passive affair, and the knower, thus construed as the "self," is understood to be fundamentally passive. When it is then admitted that this passive cognizer is also the agent who performs voluntary acts, a seeming paradox—at least a bifurcation—results. On the one hand there is passivity; on the other, activity. Why should the "self" be fundamentally passive in one area and active in the other? The notion of human presence is meant to avoid this duality. In knowing as well as doing, human presence is a dynamic and energetic item. Human presence is not merely a cognitive phenomenon. It possesses agency as well that is not another separate dimension of presence, but is fused with cognition into one inseparable thrust: the cognito-active presenting and being present to itself of human presence. This dimension or presence—presence as a dynamic energy field—is perhaps best illustrated by the phenomenon of dramatic presence. We say of an actor or actress that he or she has presence, knowing full well unthematically what we mean. Similarly, we have an understanding of what is meant by stating that someone has made himself felt as a real presence. What is needed, obviously, is a careful explication of this phenomenon and it is toward this end that this study is directed.

> As a group, they seem listless, apathetic, without drive. They could neither get themselves into things nor find a way of making those things relevant to their concerns.

illustrates a number of points. Lack of drive, a common phenomenon, is clearly one of the indicators of a deficiency in power, of a low eros-rate in human presence. Again, it requires a certain level of eros for a human presence to get into things—for it to make itself felt *as* a presence—and to find the relevance of items to the purposes and concerns of that human presence. Put another way, possessive and absorptive drives presuppose for their dynamic and intertwined development a certain level of energy, a certain eros-rate.

There is a certain, more or less definite, model for understanding the structures and dynamics of human presence. I shall refer to this model, not altogether arbitrarily, as the dialectical model for comprehending human world$_{\mathrm{H}}$s. The model finds expression in various forms in the literature of religion, philosophy, and psychoanalysis. Its essence consists in the interpretation of human presence—man—as something which both knows itself and at the same time must hide its knowledge of itself from itself.[3] The knowing is presupposed in the behavior that exhibits the hiding and the hiding is viewed as symptomatic of the knowing. Neither "self"-knowledge nor "self"-deception is understood to be accidental—the two are viewed as most intimately related.

One expression of the dialectical model is to be found in Freud, in particular, his doctrine of the unconscious. The term, "unconscious," applies to an item if two conditions are satisfied: (1) the item must be inaccessible to consciousness, permanently or at a given moment—that is to say, it must be something of which we are unaware; and (2) the item must comprise part of our knowledge, a part we do not know that we possess. Unconscious, thus, is an ambiguous term. It can apply to an item or various characteristics of that item that we know, but that we are unaware that we know. On the other hand, it can also apply to our knowledge of this item or its characteristics, knowledge that we do not know that we possess.

---

[3]The identification of man with human presence requires considerable explanation—possible only within the context of a discussion of human presence. The groundwork for this discussion is not yet laid however. Suffice it to say that "man" introduces personal notions and that "human presence" is essentially a pre-personal notion. The identity of man and human presence, thus, is an identity in difference. The stress, however, needs to be put on the identity.

What is unconscious, Freud thinks, is basic to the dynamics of both dream and waking life. For the most part, it is repressed in conscious moments and censored into unrecognizable form in its manifestation in dreams. To the extent that we draw near it, we resist it. Note that the concepts of censorship, resistance, and repression are, in the phenomenological sense, intentional in nature. They all take objects. Linguistically conceived, this means that they transform into transitive, intentional verbs which, in taking accusatives, indicate the presence of that which is their negative intent to censor, resist, or repress. Broadly speaking, the function of all three is to conceal.

For something to be concealed, however, it must first be revealed, its revelation posing a threat to the one who subsequently conceals it. Needless to say, "first" and "subsequently" function as transcendental rather than temporal terms. For Freud, thus, revelation and concealment go hand-in-hand, their dialectical interaction circumscribing the functional limits, and thus the privately owned, interpersonally accessible battleground of man as man.

Freud perhaps is not a good example to use in this primarily linguistico-phenomenological (descriptive) study. In his labors, he makes use of the dialectical model, providing an opportunity to show how widespread the model is, but he himself conceives his work as scientific and speculative, rather than descriptive.

> . . . there is one thing more which I might impress upon you: keep in mind, as a model, the method by which we have studied these phenomena. You can perceive from these examples what the aim of our psychology is. Our purpose is not merely to describe and classify the phenomena, but to conceive them as brought about by the play of forces in the mind, as expressions of tendencies striving towards a goal, which work together or against one another. We are endeavoring to attain a *dynamic conception* of mental phenomena. In this conception, the trends we merely infer are more prominent than the phenomena we perceive.[4]

Whether Freud's labors are as unphenomenological as he suggests is doubtful. This question need not detain us, however. There is another

----

[4]See Sigmund Freud, *A General Introduction to Psychoanalysis*, tr. by Joan Riviere (New York, 1962) 70-71.

thinker to consider who perhaps functions better for illustrative purposes.

In contrast to Freud, Heidegger claims phenomenological status for his account of the dynamics of a human world$_H$. His account, nonetheless, has essential resemblances to Freud's, for Heidegger also employs the dialectical model. The doctrine that results constitutes what might be termed the "existentialist" world view.[5] For Heidegger, an act of understanding, transcendentally prior to man, projects a fundamental function.[6] This function is laid before a pre-human item. In terms of it, this item comes to be aware of itself, which allows human presence to come into being. At the same conceptual moment—for here we are talking about a transcendental or conceptual rather than a temporal order of affairs—a human world$_H$ is created. What results from the act of understanding is the coming into being of man as man. Without a world$_H$, of course, there would be no man, for a world$_H$ functions transcendentally within the structure of human presence as one of its indispensable components.

In this, Heidegger is correct in his account, although incomplete. The manner in which a man relates to the function that first constitutes his world$_H$ and the manner in which he is aware of his world$_H$ itself, Heidegger holds, determine the way in which the items within that man's world$_H$ are experienced, including the man himself as "subject" of his experience.[7] It follows then that if a man relates dialectically to this fundamental function or to the world$_H$ it constitutes, all items which he experiences will be understood dialectically as well. Add to this that Heidegger's view of these two determining factors, the fundamental function and the world$_H$ it constitutes, are not altogether independent of one another and the skeletal structure of Heidegger's account is com-

---

[5]That Heidegger is not an existentialist is clear, but there is an existentialist dimension to his thought. In this connection, see my "Martin Heidegger," *Review of Metaphysics*, 19:462-92.

[6]"Function," of course, is my *terminus technicus* for "meaning." Thus, one might say that a fundamental meaning is projected.

[7]For a discussion of the notion of a man as being *within* his world$_H$, see chapter 3.

plete. Heidegger contends that the manner in which a person relates to the function that first constitutes his world$_H$ determines in large measure that person's awareness of his world$_H$. It determines most fundamentally one's experience of items within one's world$_H$ including oneself as agent of one's intentional acts. If a person relates to this function dialectically, he must relate dialectically to his world$_H$ and to the items within it as well.

Heidegger does hold that a man relates dialectically to his fundamental function—death. "Death," however, is used by Heidegger in an unusual way. It is a *terminus technicus*. Death is not understood as an event that will transpire sometime or other. Rather, Heidegger construes it as the possibility of a person having no more possibilities—of having no more functions, either in and for himself, or at his disposal aspects of such items with which he deals. When functions are no longer available to a person, he is no longer an agent. Neither does he possess awareness nor human presence, for the concepts of agency and awareness presuppose each other and, together, the notion of human presence. In this, too, Heidegger is correct, though incomplete in his account. Whether man has a fundamental function and whether, if so, it is death, are other questions—highly volatile ones.

When realized, the possibility of having no more possibilities is the extinction of man. One's fundamental possibility, in other words, is the possibility of one's no longer being at all. Therefore, death comes to be construed by Heidegger, correctly I believe, as the absence of human presence. To be sure, in saying this, one gives death a special, not-so-ordinary sense.

To speak of a man's manner of relating to his fundamental function, according to Heidegger, is to speak of the way in which a man is aware, and how he faces the awareness that his mediated reflexivity, and thus his own human presence, may at any time be extinguished. How a man relates to the ever-present possibility that this fundamental function (death) will be realized defines the nature and quality of his existence. Since man relates to this function dialectically, he is himself dialectical. Not only does Heidegger hold this view, he construes it as transcending the confines of empirical psychology.

A number of Heidegger's assertions make it clear that, in his view, it is essential to man that he hide full awareness of his fundamental function from himself.[8] For Heidegger then, a man both understands himself in the light of this fundamental function and flees from this understanding, turns away from it, or covers it up. In short, he evades it. This, of course, constitutes the essence of the dialectical model.

Like the concepts of censorship, resistance, and repression, Heideggerian notions such as flight, covering up, turning away, and evasion are, in the phenomenological sense, intentional, too. They also take objects, for they transform into transitive, intentional verbs like their Freudian counterparts. In taking accusatives or datives, these verbs indicate the presence of what their negative intent entails that their extragrammatical subjects flee from, cover up, turn away from, or evade. The function of all of these notions, in short, is to bring about concealment. Again, however, for something to be concealed, it must first be revealed. Beyond this, its revelation must pose a threat to the one who subsequently conceals it. Here, as before, "first" and "subsequently" function transcendentally.

For Heidegger, as we have seen, one's manner of relating to one's fundamental function determines in large measure the character of one's world$_H$. As an "in terms of which" or basic posture, one's world$_H$ both reveals and conceals. Revelation and concealment occur simultaneously and sustain a dialectical relation to each other.

Concerning Heidegger's variation of the dialectical model, much is obviously questionable. What I do not question, however, is the validity of the model itself, of which Heidegger's and Freud's accounts are the two most influential secular variations. Whatever the ultimate analysis of the model, human experience exhibits it too pervasively for it to be denied.

A third major expression of the dialectical model, the last one I shall mention, is found in the Judaeo-Christian religion. In adumbrating the model, the language of this religion is extremely subtle. For that which we simultaneously reveal and conceal to ourselves, it substitutes the conception of all items, including ourselves, as known by God. God's

---

[8]See Martin Heidegger, *Sefn und Zeit* (Tubingen, 1957) g.251-52, e.295-96. The English edition to which I refer is the Macquarrie and Robinson translation. See *Being and Time*, tr. by John Macquarrie and Edward Robinson (New York, 1962). The page numbers in the German edition are denoted by g., in the English by e.

knowledge, unlike ours, is said to be completely undistorted. Only in the light of God's knowledge is human knowledge possible. God's knowledge, thus, is construed as a fundamental act of revelation. With respect to the capacity of humans to reveal items, God's act of revelation is given transcendental status. For the inescapable tendencies of men to conceal items from themselves, the language of Judaeo-Christian religion substitutes the conception of sin. Sin, original and unavoidable, is understood as the act of turning away from God and his fundamental revelation. Sin, therefore, is the process of concealment. Man, it is claimed, cannot exist apart from God. Only where there is God's fundamental revelation can there be human revealing, and this revealing is presupposed by and presupposes human concealing.

The unity of human revealing and concealing is central to the concept of man. From these notions follow many other major anthropological doctrines of Judaeo-Christian religion. All of them operate within the dialectical model. They must be construed in the light of the doctrine that man is his awareness of himself—more particularly, that as human presence, he is, in part, that awareness cognate of being within himself: God is closer to us than we are to ourselves. When we flee him, we flee ourselves, and when we flee ourselves, we flee him. We cannot find God without finding ourselves, but we cannot find ourselves without finding him. When redeemed, we remain, in Luther's words, *simul justus et peccator* (simultaneously justified and yet sinners). In short, we continue both to reveal and to conceal, doing so with dialectical necessity. As human beings, we see through a glass darkly, concealing fundamental revelations of ourselves from ourselves. Never is God looked upon directly. Man flees God, but God pursues.

The languages of Freud, Heidegger, theology, and religion are not altogether consistent, being sometimes artificial and therefore abstruse. But they are no less insightful because of this. Ordinary language, on the other hand, exhibits the dialectical model by simpler means. Representative statements are not difficult to find.

He was fooling himself about his chances.

Some things are hard to admit to oneself.

I guess I've been deceiving myself about the situation for a long time.

She even hides from herself.

He just couldn't bring himself to face up to his responsibilities.

I was running from myself and I knew it.

The dialectical model is seen to pervade human experience. Its essence, as I have indicated, consists in the view that a man's fundamental posture toward items presupposes both their revelation and their concealment. Revelation makes concealment at once both possible and necessary. Concealment presupposes revelation as its indispensable transcendental prerequisite. The key to the model's dynamics is found in its conception of a man's basic posture toward himself. The manner in which a man's world$_H$ reveals him to himself, the model suggests, determines the way in which other items are revealed to him. Since a man's world$_H$ reveals him to himself dialectically, other items are revealed dialectically also.

All of these doctrines I believe to be true. What constitutes a perspicuous analysis of them, however, is another matter. In any case, an account of human presence would not be complete without taking its dialectical reflexivity into consideration. Inspection of reflexivity leads in turn to a consideration of the "self," for the reflexive dimension of human presence is to some degree constitutive of the "self." Problematic reflexivity is the locus and source of a particular sort of distortion—self-deception. Self-deception involves, as its necessary condition, human presence relating to itself distortedly.

Herbert Fingarette has an account of self-deception that is immensely helpful with regard to understanding both self-deception and the "self" which is so deceived.[9] His discussion illuminates human reflexivity considerably and, therefore, human presence. Since, as I have argued, world$_H$s must be understood in accordance with the dialectical model—a model that has self-deception at its base—a critical analysis of Fingarette's position is very much in order, and not only on this account. Philosophers in the tradition have evidenced considerable concern regarding the existence and characteristics of the "self." Yet this concern has not issued in any clear and commonly accepted account of it, either with respect to its existence or nature. In the course of my discussion, I shall introduce a line of thought that may lead to the remedying of this situation. My major aim remains the same, however: the illumination of

---

[9]See Herbert Fingarette, *Self-Deception* (New York 1969).

human presence, of which the "self," human reflexivity, and self-deception are basic dimensions.

Fingarette distinguishes two different sets of terms: those from the cognition/perception family and those from the volition/action family. He claims that self-deception has usually been understood by means of cognition/perception terminology and that terms such as "appear," "see," "perceive," "consciousness," and "awareness" have been used to explicate the phenomenon of self-deception. Fingarette's strategy is in two parts: (1) to isolate conscious and its variants and to show that they would be more perspicuously treated as members of the volition/action family; and (2) to develop on this basis a volition/action account of self-deception.

The importance of Fingarette's effort is far broader than its application to situations involving self-deception, however. Generally speaking, the Western philosophical tradition has construed the essential difference between man and "lower" forms of life to be the possession of and special character of human consciousness. This term, consciousness, has been construed as the passive capacity to absorb and assimilate information upon which to base action. Man, in short, has been understood in terms of his capacity for knowledge and knowing has been understood passively. "Seeing," a word indicating the passive capacity to assimilate visual information, has, in fact, been the paradigm term. Man, it is claimed, receives information. More generally, consciousness is the receptor to which information comes (often via the senses). It is also the passive receptacle in which this information is stored.

Fingarette's account of consciousness, not altogether unlike Heidegger, Merleau-Ponty, and Wittgenstein, does not sanction this passive doctrine. To be conscious involves an act or series of acts. Explicit consciousness is the exercise of a skill. As Fingarette indicates, one may either refuse or resolve to become explicitly conscious of something. Such explicit consciousness can be attained either effectively or ineffectively, carelessly or conscientiously, and for bad or good reasons. The capacity to become, with care and skill, explicitly conscious in one area does not necessarily entail a developed capacity to become explicitly conscious in another. The conscious skill involved in being able to identify various sorts of birds, for instance, meaning the ability to be aware of them, may go hand-in-hand with an undeveloped, perhaps marginal, capacity for being conscious of subtle differences in tonal variations.

Let us translate these notions over into the developing rubric of human presence, world$_H$s, and views. To view a particular subject matter is, paradigmatically, to exercise a certain skill with respect to that subject matter: the skill of articulating it into its component parts and their interrelations, and then ordering these parts and interrelations in terms of their relative importance for one's purposes and propensities for enjoyment. Having different purposes and propensities for enjoyment, various agents will view a subject matter differently. What is open to a given agent's view depends upon four factors: (1) the skill that the agent has developed with respect to the subject matter to be articulated; (2) the agent's purposes; (3) the agent's propensities for enjoyment; and (4) the amount of effort the agent chooses to put into the exercise of his skill at the time that the subject matter is available to him. Note the distinction between the second and third factors. By purposes is meant the possessive thrust of eros; by propensities, the enjoyment, the absorptive thrust. These two factors are always intermixed, however, and their separation into distinct components is but a convenient abstraction. In any case, these four factors determine one's view, and differences in these factors among individual agents—or of the same agent at different times—are reflected in how what is viewed is actually articulated and ultimately seen.

A capacity to view one sort of thing, perhaps a landscape, need not indicate a skill of equal magnitude in viewing, say, human relationships. Even within one field of view and with respect to one agent, there may be uneven viewing skill and, therefore, an uneven view. Take as an example human relationships. A man may be very skilled at viewing and subsequently dealing with rivalries and jealousies, but he may be extremely unskilled in viewing and coping with apathies and indifferences.

A total field of view is made up of many different overlapping, perhaps sometimes conflicting, exercises of viewing skills. Fields of view are the result of the exercisings of skills that have developed to various degrees. These fields are the results, too, of the varying amounts of energy invested in the operation of the various skills. Energy investment is a function of eros-rate and eros-rate is determined to no small degree by the possessive/absorptive balance of an agent as it is reflected in his purposes and propensities for enjoyment. Like views, perspectives must be understood to be subject to the same factors.

A world$_H$ must be construed in terms of the same factors as views and perspectives. One's world$_H$ is fundamentally a complex act, namely, the exercising of a number of different skills that may well oppose each other. The result of exercising these skills is viewing our world in a different sense; involving those inner-worldly items that one confronts, becomes part of, possesses, and deals with to varying degrees. This means that a world$_H$ is an active "in terms of which," because it issues forth as a plurality of modes of activity and a multiplicity of exercised skills. Its result is a world of inner-worldly items in interrelation with ourselves in which we are bound. A world$_H$'s eros-rate is the degree to which and the manner in which energy is expended in those possessive and absorptive acts that are the direct expression of skills. In every case, skills have possessive and absorptive possibilities and every exercise of a skill expresses the balance between the two drives in one way or another. The drives are always mixed in with one another in any given act. The distinction between these two drives, however, is fundamental to the comprehension of skills, their exercise, and employment.

I have referred to human presence as an act in the Aristotelian sense as a means of capturing the non-passive aspect of this presence. The uniqueness of human presence is noted primarily in the capacity to do something rather than in the capacity to undergo something. One of the acts that human presence performs is that of presenting itself to the items that it encounters, and articulating this encounter so that those items may be present to it. "Self"-presentation and articulation may be carried out with varying degrees of eros and the manner of possessive/absorptive balance varying widely.

Fingarette construes explicit consciousness to be the exercising of a certain skill. The specific skill that serves as his model for comprehending the act of becoming explicitly conscious is the skill of saying what one is experiencing or doing. He calls this skill spelling out. Statements such as the following clearly illustrate the relevance of such terminology.

Can't you see what I'm doing? Do I have to spell it out for you?

If you're unable to catch the nuances of the movement, I'll spell them out for you in detail.

Just to make sure you understand the sort of intervention that is required, I'll spell it out for you step by step.

He's pretty intuitive in catching on to what's expected of him, but some things you have to spell out for him in minute detail.

"Spelling out" for Fingarette is roughly equivalent to "making explicit." He also construes spelling out to be closely analogous to linguistic activity.

Given its close analogy to linguistic activity, Fingarette's notion of spelling out can best be understood through reference to what I have elsewhere termed intelligibility-articulation.[10] Intelligibility-articulation is neither written nor spoken. It is the prelinguistic act of making manifest or bringing out into the open that which is to be dealt with in such a way that everything that comes to be recognized, done, and/or said about it is drawn from the subject itself. A distinguishing feature of human presence, intelligibility-articulation is that by which human presence brings itself into the presence of items in such a way that what comes to be recognized, done, and/or said about these items can be derived from these items themselves. In short, through intelligibility-articulation, human presence makes itself present to inner-worldly items and vice versa. Intelligibility-articulation is the articulate and, thus cognitive, manifestation of eros.[11]

Fingarette claims that people are engaged in the world in a variety of different ways. For him these engagements are a person's various doings and undergoings, activities and projects. Their sum total constitute one's world at a given time. World, of course, must be construed as one's "in terms of which" together with those inner-worldly items and situations articulated in terms of it. The thesis Fingarette urges is that both the general and particular features of people's engagements are, for the most part, not spelled out by them. Stated somewhat differently, people are generally not explicitly conscious of their engagements—their reasons, motives, aims, attitudes, and feelings, and the worldly and in-

---

[10]See my *Language and Being: An Analytic Phenomenology* (New Haven and London, 1970) 98ff. See also 45ff of this chapter.

[11]To my knowledge, Fingarette has no doctrine of presence nor of eros. What I present here, thus, is Fingarette's spelling-out doctrine phrased in language amenable to my investigations in *Language and Being* and to my present investigation into human presence.

ner-worldly items to which these relate through understanding and action.

Fingarette urges that (1) there must be a reason for spelling out; (2) since not everything can be spelled out, spelling out is a selective process; (3) the use of the spelling-out skill involves an initial assessment of the appropriate engagement situation to determine whether there exists a reason to spell out or, for that matter a reason not to spell out; and (4) since spelling-out is itself a mode of engagement, it is not spelled out unless there exists a special reason for doing so.

These doctrines can profitably be translated into the language of human presence, for it is by nature dispersed into a set of simultaneous and successive worldly and inner-worldly concerns. A few of these concerns are subjected to actual intelligibility-articulation. To speak of human presence's dispersion into a set of concerns is to say that human presence is diversified, manifested to varying degrees in the various pursuits undertaken and experiences undergone by human beings. Human presence's dispersion is in some areas primarily possessive, in others primarily absorptive. The degree of energy with which human presence manifests itself varies from pursuit to pursuit and experience to experience. In some of its concerns, this presence is intensely involved, in others but slightly. The eros-rate is highly differentiated. Further, the unity of human presence in the midst of its concrete, worldly, and inner-worldly immersion is more a task than a given. Perhaps it has the unity ascribed by Kant to his transcendental unity of apperception. Empirically, however, it is clear that such a unity is threadbare in the face of the multiple ways in which human presence is engaged with worldly and inner-worldly items. To the degree that the "self" is construed as the reflexive and unified character of human presence, the unity of the "self" and its identity over time are problematic. Whether the "self" should be construed as that unity of human presence brought about by a single or set of reflexive moves and what such moves actually are certainly are questions in their own right.

Fingarette's remarks concerning spelling out are easily applicable to intelligibility-articulation.[12] There must be a reason for intelligibility-articulation if it is to be carried out. This exercise is a selective process,

---

[12]See in this connection the last chapter of this study.

for its activity cannot encompass all of human presence's diversified concerns. For intelligibility-articulation to take place, there must first be an assessment of the appropriate manifestation of human presence to determine whether there exists a reason either to engage in the exercise or not. Finally, since intelligibility-articulation is a mode of human presence's concern, it is itself not subject to intelligibility-articulation unless there exists a special reason for so doing.

Fingarette's account of self-deception follows directly from his remarks concerning explicit consciousness and spelling-out. Human beings are engaged in and with their world in various ways, meaning they have a number of engagements. In cases of self-deception, however, there exists a prevailing reason not to engage in spelling out some particular engagement. The man who falls into self-deception takes this reason into account on the basis that he refrains from spelling out the relevant engagement. His avoidance of such spelling-out, in fact, is systematic. Not only this, the man refrains from spelling out his decision not to exercise his skill in spelling out with respect to the engagement in question. In Fingarette's account, it is this set of circumstances that constitutes self-deception. Stated another way, there is an avoidance of becoming explicitly conscious of an engagement and a further avoidance of becoming explicitly conscious that the avoidance has indeed taken place. Note Fingarette's further claim that spelling out is an activity that an agent must do for himself; to spell out is to do so in terms of one's world. If another person spells something out for someone else, it is in terms of *his* world, not the other's world, that the spelling out takes place. Herein lies a large measure of the truth in the individualistic thrust of existentialism. There are, after all, certain things that a man can only do himself and for himself.

Before further modifying and translating Fingarette's account into the language of human presence, let us consider it in more detail. Fingarette claims that a person in self-deception persistently desists from spelling out some engagement or feature of an engagement in the world—even though it would normally be appropriate for him to spell it out. In fact, from an outsider's vantage point, it looks and becomes construed as if the person in self-deception were unable to admit the truth. It looks as if he were not able to articulate and make explicit certain dimensions of his doings and undergoings. But, as Fingarette claims, stating the matter in this way can be misleading. The inability indicates no lack of strength or skill. Rather, this inability is the expression of a person's adherence to a policy tacitly adopted. It is because of a policy not to spell something out that the person in self-deception does not spell it out and falls into self-deception. The person in self-deception is in a curious circumstance indeed—he fails to spell something out, though he gives the impression that he could, appearing that he has rendered himself incapable of spelling that item out because of an adopted policy.

It follows, therefore, that the reasons for refusing to spell some engagement out must themselves not be spelled out. If they were, the engagement(s) to be masked would be spelled out in the process. To articulate the reasons for not spelling out an engagement, after all, would require reference to the engagement not to be spelled out. This would defeat the original purpose of the refusal to spell out, namely the hiding and/or denial of the relevant engagement. The policy not to spell something out, thus, is, in Fingarette's terms, a self-covering policy. It is not itself articulated. Three results emerge from this circumstance. First, there are gaps in the normal range of the self-deceiver's spellings out as the hidden area is approached. Second, cover stories are usually created to hide the discrepancies and gaps in spellings out engendered by self-deception and its self-covering policies. Third, a discrepancy arises in the activities of the person involved in self-deception—how he engages himself and what he says. In short, questions of sincerity arise.

Fingarette distinguishes between the individual and the person. The individual is construed as that set of engagements that constitutes a man's active life of doings and undergoings. To be a person, however, involves something more. It requires the avowal of these engagements. To avow an engagement or set of engagements is to acknowledge that engagement as one's own, and identify oneself with it. To the extent that a man does this, he is a person. Fingarette construes personal identity, therefore, as a task to be accomplished. Avowals which either acknowledge or create engagements are its building blocks. Disavowal of one's engagements, on the other hand, constitutes an unwillingness to accept oneself as is, denying one's personal identity.

Fingarette distinguishes those engagements that are intrinsic to a person's identity at a given time from those that are not in terms of the person's capacity to spell out his engagements. Those that can be spelled out constitute one's identity as a person. Capacity to spell out an engagement indicates that the engagement has been avowed, and this avowal of engagements constitutes personal identity. Engagements that are not avowed, on the other hand, cannot be spelled out; for in failing to avow them, one surrenders one's authority—and, in a curious way, one's capacity—to spell them out.

Fingarette claims there is a mark that usually distinguishes disavowed engagements from avowed ones: disavowed engagements are usually isolated from the influence of those engagements that are avowed. Disavowed engagements neither influence nor are influenced by avowed ones. In contrast, personal identity and the harmony and sophistication of "personality" involve the continuous and mutual influence of avowed engagements upon one another. Disavowed engagements are set apart from this system of mutual influence, remaining relatively static and underdeveloped. This circumstance stands in sharp contrast to the situation in which personal identity is found. Where there is personal identity, a variety of diverse engagements are acknowledged as belonging together, acted upon, and effort is made to make these avowed engagements coalesce into harmony and unity.

I have gone into Fingarette's account in some detail because it provides a useful model for construing some of the basic dimensions of human presence. Such presence finds itself dispersed into a variety of worldly and inner-worldly concerns, being engaged in multiple ways. Talk of a basic and transcendental unity of consciousness often leads to the disregard of this circumstance. Such disregard is quite misleading, for in actual fact, human presence presents itself to its world and the included items in a variety of concurrently differing ways. Human presence can simultaneously be presenting itself to and making present to itself this item in one way, that item in another, both thematically or unthematically. More often than not there are differential eros-rates involved and differing possessive/absorptive balances within the rich fabric of any of human presence's manifestation at a given time. The doctrine of the unity of consciousness fails to highlight these facts. Moreover, the doctrine is usually tied to a conception of consciousness as fundamentally cognitive, and cognitive in a detached and scientific manner—witness Kant, the Tractarian Wittgenstein, and the early Husserl. In contrast to this consciousness model, human presence must be construed as a complex, multidirectional affair that acts and reacts, does and undergoes in disparate though concurrent ways that merge, emerge, come into conflict, and achieve harmony over time.

Fingarette's account of self-deception bears close resemblance to the dialectical model for understanding human world$_H$s presented in the first chapter. Fingarette's account, however, is developed further. Paradoxically, this is a source both of its strength and of its weakness. Consider again the dialectical model. This model construes human presence as something that both knows itself and at the same time must hide this self- knowledge from itself. Human presence's knowledge of itself is presupposed by this behavior. Human presence's hiding of its "self"-knowledge is construed as a symptomatic reaction to "self"-knowledge. In seeming contrast, Fingarette struggles to overcome any fundamentally cognitive conception of self-deception, any conception that would construe self-deception as both the possession of and rejection of some piece of knowledge about the self. At the very least he attempts to construe self-deception in accordance with the volition/action family of concepts rather than the perception/cognition family. Fingarette's way of accomplishing his purpose is first to construe human beings as engaged in their worlds in a multiplicity of different ways, having a variety of differing engagements. These engagements involve skills both in doing and undergoing.

One is tempted to say, "so far, so good," for when translated into the language of human presence, Fingarette's account of this point appears to be without flaw. Human presence is involved with worldly and inner-worldly items in multiple ways. Given the purposive orientation of human agency and the inextricability of agency considerations from any account of awareness and, thus, human presence, the involvements of this presence must be construed as purposive, as engaged, rather than as disinterested and (cognitively) detached. Human presence's involvements clearly are manifestations of skills that may either be active or passive. In any case, these skills and their manifestations are ineradicably purposive—in other words, they have differential possessive/absorptive thrust.

Fingarette's next step is the difficult one. He claims that in cases of self-deception there exists a strong reason not to spell out a particular engagement. This reason is taken into account, acted upon, and the engagement is in fact not spelled out. Further, both the reason and the decision for not spelling it out, a decision based on this reason, are themselves not spelled out. For Fingarette, it is this set of circumstances that captures the essence of self-deception. The apparent flaw in Fingarette's account arises from his assertion that a reason exists for not spelling an engagement out and, further, that the person practicing self-deception acts upon this reason. To have a reason for not spelling out an engagement is to know both that one has a reason and what the reason is. One must necessarily connect the reason with the engagement not to be spelled out. It follows, therefore, that if one is to refrain from spelling out an engagement, one must know what this engagement is. One's reason must relate to the engagement in question, and the engagement in question must be both known and connected with the reason. By Fingarette's own account, self-deception must involve both knowing and not knowing. One must both know the engagement not to be spelled out—how else would one know that the engagement is not to be spelled out?—and fail to know the engagement not to be spelled out. The obvious problem is to comprehend how this paradox is not only an abstract possibility but a part of the fabric of actual life.

Consider now the circumstance of self-deception when put in the language of human presence. This presence is dispersed into a variety of concurrent possessive/absorptive doings and undergoings that transpire at differential eros-rates. Some of these doings and undergoings have been subjected to considerable intelligibility-articulation; some have not. With respect to any particular engagement, there are in fact three possibilities: (1) it has not been subjected to intelligibility-articulation; (2) it has been subjected to intelligibility-articulation but has not been expressed linguistically; and (3) it has been both subjected to intelligibility-articulation and expressed linguistically. It appears, therefore, as if cases of self-deception can be of two sorts. Either an engagement satisfies the first condition, but not the second and third, or it satisfies the second condition, but not the first or third.

This account is not without its difficulties, however. It is especially questionable given the validity of the argument establishing that self-deception involves a person's knowledge of that which he deceives himself. How can there be knowledge whose object is totally free of intelligibility-articulation? More specifically, how can the first condition be satisfied, yet involve an engagement or concern as an object of knowledge? Knowledge entails mediation. Intelligibility-articulation is the most fundamental, the most basic, mediating agency, being presupposed by all other mediating elements. If self-deception truly involves knowledge of that which a person deceives himself, either the satisfaction of the first condition, but not the second and third, fails to constitute a genuine case of self-deception or there is knowledge that circumvents mediation.

The solution to this problem lies in construing the first condition, when a particular engagement is in no way subjected to intelligibility-articulation, as a limiting condition. Though many engagements may closely approximate to total freedom from intelligibility-articulation, no engagement actually achieves this freedom. At least one form of self-deception involves an engagement's minimal intelligibility-articulation, a sense that if such an exercise was carried out further, unhappy circumstances would arise, and a decision would be made not to engage in further intelligibility-articulation. What constitutes minimal intelligibility-articulation will differ from situation to situation. It is always relative and a matter of degree. In a given circumstance a great deal of intelligibility-articulation may yet be minimal, in terms of the full circumstance. If there is a common factor, it is the sense that if intelligibility-articulation is carried out further, certain features and consequences of one or more concerns of human presence will be brought to light and will be unhappy.

But what exactly is this "sense?" Stated this way, the question cannot be answered, at least not straightforwardly. A sense that such-and-such would be the case is precisely the sort of thing that cannot be subjected to complete intelligibility-articulation, and complete intelligibility-articulation, in turn, is precisely the model in which a straightforward answer is construed. Yet, most everyone is familiar with the type of sense that is under consideration here unless, of course, he has been corrupted by philosophical coyness. Consider the following statements. They embody the term, sense, and its variants in ways closely analogous, if not identical, with the use now in question.

He had a sense of impending doom.

Having sensed that he was angry, she decided not to make her request until the next day.

He sensed that something was wrong but couldn't put his finger on it.

Her sense of propriety was offended, but she could detect no specific cause.

He sensed that he was in trouble.

These statements, together with variations on them, are quite familiar. They adumbrate familiar circumstances. A person may sense something to be the case but be wrong. People who have a sense of catastrophe or impending doom are often thought to be ill and in need of professional attention. People often sense something about themselves, act upon what they sense, and yet are totally unable to explain or even comprehend for themselves exactly what they sense. It is this latter group that merits attention in connection with the phenomenon of self-deception. For human presence to enter into self-deception is for it to sense that one or more of its concerns, if subjected to (further) intelligibility-articulation, would lead it into an unhappy state of affairs. Sensing this, human presence does not subject the concern(s) in question to further intelligibility-articulation. Plus, human presence's sense that an unhappy state of affairs would result is itself left vague and unarticulated. Perhaps the problematic concern is subjected to an alternative, distorting intelligibility-articulation; perhaps it is subjected to a cover story. Yet, the problematic concern and human presence's sense of its problematic nature may simply be left as is—not subjected to intelligibility-articulation to any further degree than they have already been subjected. In any case, human presence continues to pursue the concern(s) in question and these circumstances capture the essence of self-deception.

It is possible that Fingarette's account is compatible with the account that I have just offered. He claims there must be a reason for not spelling out an engagement. I have claimed there must be a sense that intelligibility-articulation would lead to unhappy circumstances. If Fingarette's conception of a reason is equivalent to my notion of a sense, there probably is no genuine disagreement between the two accounts. I suspect by "reason," however, he wishes to indicate something more transparent and rational than I intend by the word. Fortunately for the matter at hand, this question's resolution is not imperative.

A matter that must be further resolved, however, concerns the notion of unhappy circumstances. I have claimed that the desire to avoid knowledge of unhappy circumstances is what motivates human presence not to subject certain of its concerns, its possessive/absorptive doings and undergoings, to intelligibility-articulation. But knowledge of precisely what sort of unhappy circumstances is to be avoided? Does the desire to avoid any sort of unhappy circumstance that would arise from subjecting a concern to intelligibility-articulation qualify as a motive for self-deception? These are difficult questions.

The two most prevalent explanations of the unhappy circumstance, the knowledge of which is to be avoided, and the motive for self-deception come from existentialism and psychiatry. Some existentialists claim that a man is what he does and undergoes, that he is his engagements. Further, they argue, it is in man's nature to be engaged in bringing about the end of all his engagements. This engagement, primarily undergone rather than done, is referred to as death. If a man is his engagements, and one of his engagements is to undergo the dissolution of all his engagements, then man is engaged in bringing about his own termination as man. Of every man, these existentialists claim, two things can be said in this regard: he will succeed in undergoing this engagement-extinguishing engagement, and only he can undergo it.

So painful is this engagement-ending engagement, it is argued, that men must conceal their possession of it from themselves. To know that life is an engagement in dying, in terminating all engagements, is virtually unbearable. Much of the pain lies in the fact that this engagement is difficult, perhaps impossible, for a man to integrate with his other engagements. In pointing toward the ultimate eclipse of other engagements, it is a source of discord rather than harmony in the engagement matrix. This discord among engagements, it is claimed, is a (if not *the*) fundamental source of agony. To be one's engagements and to have discord among them is to be torn apart. (Note that the existentialists who describe and assess death in accordance with the account I have given hold for the most part that, as an engagement, death can be known and integrated. To do so is to attain authenticity.)

There are many schools of psychiatric thought concerning the locus and dynamics of unhappy circumstances, so many, in fact, that it is virtually impossible to generalize here. Rather than trying to distill a common essence, I shall present schematically what might be termed the classical model. Variations on this model bear enough family resemblance to be covered or at least suggested, albeit obliquely, through its explication. The classical model postulates various repressed wishes and desires. Construe these as engagements neither explicitly nor straightforwardly acted out or upon. Alternatively, they may be construed as those concerns of human presence that have a high degree of eros invested in them, but in which human presence avoids making itself present to as much degree as it finds possible. Why are these engagements not acted out? Why does human presence attempt, unsuccessfully, to withdraw itself from these concerns? Civilization and/or society, it is said, imposes conditions that deny to men the opportunity to act out these repressed engagements or concerns. These societal conditions become internalized standards, self-policing engagements in their own right that are further reinforced by additional commerce with one's fellows. The result of this internalization is that two sets of concerns stand in opposition to one another: internalized concerns to act in certain "civilized" ways and primal, perhaps phylogenetically grounded, and repressed concerns (desires, wishes) to act in ways that, it is assumed, would bring immediate satisfaction. To make these latter desires explicit would be to bring to explicit consciousness engagements that cannot be acted upon without terrible conflict among one's engagements—and pain results. Not only to bring to light but to act upon these engagements would be to split the person, construed as his engagements, asunder. In either case there is engendered a most unhappy set of circumstances.

Formally at least, existentialism and a psychiatry agree that conflict among engagements is the basic source of unhappy circumstances. If one were Freudian enough to accept Freud's conclusions in *Civilization and its Discontents*, and if, further, one were Heideggerian in one's existentialism, existentialism and psychiatry would be in virtual material agreement as well—in spite of conflicting ontologies. The engagement a man undergoes with death and the difficulties in accepting it and harmonizing it with other engagements would be construed as what constituted the primary unhappy circumstance of the human condition. This doctrine I wish to endorse. Put in the language of human presence, human presence has among its concerns one with death. It must undergo this concern in the specific sense that human presence is its concern and death is an ineradicable concern. A considerable amount of eros is invested in death, yet for the most part, human presence attempts to withdraw itself from its concern with death. This it does either possessively through the act of trying to manage death or absorptively through suicidal activity. Human presence is authentic or, alternatively, healed, but only to the extent that it can pursue death openly, and integrate and harmonize the undergoing of death with its other concerns. What pursuing death openly involves requires contextual definition and is, of course, another and terribly difficult question altogether. That the question is an old and venerable one can be seen in Socrates's doctrine that philosophy is learning how to die.

To this point, self-deception has been construed as that situation in which a particular engagement, which may be understood now as death, has not been subjected to intelligibility-articulation—with the added proviso that total lack of subjection to intelligibility-articulation is a limiting case. The form of self-deception so far discussed, thus, involves the minimal intelligibility-articulation of an engagement, a sense that if this exercise were carried out further, unhappy circumstances would arise, and on this basis a decision is made not to engage in further intelligibility-articulation.

Another form of self-deception exists, however, which as yet has received only passing mention. Perhaps this is because this form is most difficult to disentangle and distinguish from the first form discussed. In this new form, a concern is subjected to intelligibility-articulation, but is not expressed linguistically. In cases such as these, linguistic expression is denied because human presence senses that such expression, in making the concern explicit, would bring about explicit pain. Linguistic expression, however, like intelligibility-articulation, must be construed as a matter of degree. The distinction between intelligibility-articulation and linguistic expression is itself subject to variations. There are times when intelligibility-articulation itself proceeds only through linguistic expression. Various emotions such as anger are cases in point. Sometimes intelligibility-articulation proceeds in relative independence of linguistic expression. Comprehension of some of the visual dimensions of art and the audio dimensions of music exemplify this type of intelligibility-articulation/language relation. ("Language" must be construed here as the phenomenon of speech, be it written, spoken, or silently spoken.) Again, there may be some linguistic expression given to an unexplicated concern, a repressed concern, but the sense that further expression would be painful hinders further linguistic "speaking out." When this situation exists, self-deception is present as well, for this situation defines a second, intimately related form of self-deception.

Having discussed self-deception, I am now able to raise again and give partial answer to three earlier questions concerning human presence. These questions were previously construed in terms of the overlapping rubric of human world$_H$s: (1) How do a human world$_H$'s extracognitive dimensions function in its dialectical structure? (2) What is the most perspicuous description of a human world$_H$'s dialectical structure? (3) How central is the concept of a fundamental function to a dialectical model of a human world$_H$? My consideration of these questions will end this chapter.

To this stage of investigation, the dialectical model has been construed primarily in cognitive terms. Thus its essence has been understood as a transcendentally simultaneous revelation and concealment. Revelation makes concealment necessary, and concealment presupposes revelation as that which generates its dynamics. This cognitive model by no means needs to be abandoned, but it must be supplemented by elements of an extracognitive model. This latter model suggests factors that may well remove cognition from its pride of primary place. But this is a misleading way of stating the matter. The cognitive and the extracognitive must not be construed as operating in functional independence of each other. To conceive their relation in this way would be to commit what might be termed the positivist fallacy—the strict bifurcation of the mental into separate compartments, together with the ascription of meaning and, potentially, truth to one compartment, and intensity or some such property to the other. Rather than accept this disguised conceptual recommendation, the cognitive and the extracognitive must be construed as intimately intertwined. Their distinction is as much for heuristic purposes as it is in the nature of things.

The concept of insight in psychotherapy illustrates this point well. To achieve insight is not simply to intellectually comprehend the truth of certain propositions. Were this the case, therapy would be very quick and very successful, given intelligent therapists and patients. Rather, what is to be known must be lived through, undergone, and, finally, undone. This process is emotional as well as intellectual—though the distinction between emotional and intellectual has lost its force in this context. Clearly, this process is not merely emotional, for in therapy emotion is tied to comprehension and alteration of behavior patterns. Mere emotional indulgence is not helpful. Insight might best be described as the skilled undergoing, undoing, and alteration of basic behavior patterns. Thought and feeling intermingle so intimately that it might be conjectured that they arise from a common human force.

How, then, do a human world$_H$'s extracognitive dimensions function in its dialectical structure? Human presence is dispersed into and manifested in a multiplicity of differing concerns. It actively engages itself in some of these concerns; others it mostly undergoes. The distinction between doing and undergoing is one of degree, not kind. These manifestations of human presence have differential eros-rates and varied possessive/absorptive balances. The level of eros commitment—one is tempted to say psychic investment—in a given concern determines the degree of intensity of that concern and the degree of human presence that the concern exhibits. Through human presence's absorptive drive, it gives itself over to its concerns, attempting fully to identify itself with them. Human presence's possessive drive motivates it to take over its concerns, master, develop, and modify them as its own. In "taking over" its concerns, as opposed to "becoming one with," human presence differentiates itself as being manipulator of these concerns. Possessive drive, thus, is a source of human presence's self-differentiation. Absorptive drive, on the other hand, is a source of human presence's nonmediated identity, an identity that Hegel termed immediacy. Note that Hegel's essentially cognitive identity in a doctrine of difference, if transformed into human presence's language, gets construed as the inextricable interrelatedness, complementarity, and conflict of possessive/absorptive drive at human presence's core.

Careful note must be taken of the situation that both manifests and is human presence. Since this presence, in part at least, is its concerns, the movement of absorptive drive is a movement toward human presence's identification of itself with itself. This movement is away from disruption in which human presence stands apart from its concerns, and toward unity in which human presence merges with its concerns, becoming one with them. Were human presence's absorptive drive to be consuming to the exclusion of possessive drive, human presence, in merging with its concerns, would be in a state of Hegelian immediacy, free of the cancer of consciousness.

This state is never attained, however, for the concerns of human presence encounter obstacles. Obstacles to human presence's concerns or, for that matter, concerns' internal difficulties be they intellectual or existential, motivate human presence to differentiate itself from these concerns. Not only this, under this set of circumstances human presence is motivated possessively to grasp its concerns, modify, and manipulate them. Such modification and manipulation constitutes human presence's self-transformation. Human presence, after all, is its concerns. To the degree that it modifies them or they undergo modification, either through accident, outside agency, or other circumstances, human presence itself is transformed. On the other hand, to the extent to which human presence merely differentiates itself from its concerns and stands apart from them, this presence is in the state of alienation. To the extent that human presence is unable either to successfully modify its concerns so as to remove obstacles to them, or successfully alter them so as to remove those internal difficulties that they possess, or merge and fuse itself with its concerns, human presence is equally alienated.

Human presence's concern with death presents it with special difficulties. Were this concern one that could be set aside, these difficulties could be overcome through renunciation of the concern. Such is not possible, however. Human presence's concern with death is abiding and must in various continual ways, large and small, be undergone until its final resolution: human presence's own final dissolution. Along with human presence's other engagements, concerns, pursuits, and undergoings, death must be integrated into harmonious and intimate interrelationships with its fellows. As an engagement undergone, death constitutes at its fruition a human presence's irrevocable absenting of itself as presence. Death, thus, constitutes the end of that human presence's individually sustained, at least partially conscious, doings and undergoings. To integrate death with other concerns is to comprehend these concerns as terminal and at some point in time to be terminated.

There are a variety of ways in which human presence can meld its concerns, many of which have no terminal dimension to their structure, into intimate interrelations with death. Consider first these two constructive ways. Human presence can channel absorptive drive into social or political movements. In this way, even though individual human presence construes itself rightly as a terminal nature, it allows some of its force—its erotic élan—to be absorbed by forces that transcend its individual life. This gives human presence a sense of union with forces more powerful than its own and a sense of continuance beyond its finite existence. For human presence to know that, in part at least, it is its own concern is to have opened to it the possibility of melding itself *qua* concerns with concerns that transcend its own individual ones. Insofar as these concerns "live on" after the actual absenting of a particular human presence (death), that presence itself lives on, but not as a conscious agency. Attachment to some transcendent concerns enable a human presence to come to terms with and accept the fusing of a terminal dimension to other of its concerns as well.

Another manner in which human presence may attempt to integrate its concern with death with its other concerns is by creating various items that, as manifestation of its concern and, thus, part of its concern, have a continued existence after human presence's final absenting. These created items embody a human presence's concern. This state of affairs is brought about rather simply. Under the influence of absorptive drive, human presence is "taken in" by the potentialities of the worldly and inner-worldly items about it. Through the (transcendentally) simultaneous manifestation of a human presence's possessive drive, these potentialities are functionally interpreted. This process of functional interpretation and its result, simultaneous with the carrying out of the process, are embodied in an artifact—a term that must be construed broadly. The artifact, in embodying a human presence's concern, manifests that presence itself. Once another human presence becomes absorbed in and by the artifact, the concern reemerges if only for a fleeting period. This reemergence is a prolongation, however episodic, of the human presence whose concern brought the artifact into being. This manner of both accepting yet transcending human presence's terminal nature is the way of the creator, be he poet or sculptor, architect, novelist, or participant in some other medium. The former manner of acceptance, yet transcendence, is the way of a political or social human presence. These two ways need not be exclusive of each other and may, in fact, complement one another.

Having explicated two relatively constructive ways of integrating death into the ongoing concerns of human presence, I am under some obligation to account for why such integration is needed at all. Why not hold to the view that death is but another fact of life? As such, it is something to be accepted as inevitable, as it will occur at some time or another. Though it will terminate one's concerns as an individual human presence, it need not stand in the way of one's other concerns. Come when it may, death need not be related to, much less disintegrate, one's present and ongoing concerns. At a human presence's final absenting of itself, some of its concerns will quite naturally be continued by others, and the others will simply come to an end. Such is the way of things.

There is much to this argument or, perhaps better termed, attitude. It sensitively states the case against various morbid and narcissistic forms of reaction to the human condition. This matter-of-fact attitude is not sufficient, however, for it fails to accept and deal with the consequences of the vital, ineradicable drive of human presence to be, rather than not to be. To recognize this drive—a recognition to be achieved through phenomenological presentation rather than by means of argumentational devices—is to further recognize the drive or concern for some form of continuance beyond the individual absenting of itself of an individual human presence. Inextricably intertwined with human presence's engagement with death is a concurrent concern for human presence's prolongation. This speaks against acceptance of merely finite concerns— concerns that terminate altogether with an individual human presence's death. To accept human presence's final absenting of itself without attempting its partial transcendence is an exercise in frustration. Quite specifically, it is the frustration of the continuance concern that is inseparably related to its concern with death.

Existentialism in some of its forms accepts this frustration. The futility of human presence is its credo. But futility is only futility as the dark shadow of a concern with continuance. Since many existentialists, in reaction to Hegel, tend to identify continuance with explicit flesh and blood continuance, they are necessarily frustrated and life for them is absurd. The radical individualism of this brand of existentialism, together with its commitment to the concrete fact of individual human presence, makes it morbid at times and allows it to characterize the human condition as without meaning. To accept both the terminal absenting of itself of human presence and the equally ineradicable concern with continuance in a constructive manner is to go beyond that form of existentialism just described. To this end I have forwarded two constructive solutions, venerable in origin and age.

There are less constructive resolutions open to human presence, however. Unfortunately, somewhat metaphorical and oblique language is required to describe them. In some instances human presence attempts to escape its concern with death by exercising its possessive drive to the end of accumulating worldly and inner-worldly items. Human presence then identifies itself with these items, construing them, however unthematically, as proof against its own termination. This activity is adumbrated by the poet, Wordsworth, when he says that worldly items are too much with men. It is also suggested by Jesus' exhortation to be in the world but not of the world. However dark these remarks and for whatever differing reasons they are made, they constitute a negative judgment against the accumulation of worldly goods and subsequent possession and identification with them. I shall introduce a special term to refer to this process of accumulation, possession, and identification—insistence. It may be helpful to note that insistence as presently defined is, in Sartre's terms, one way in which a "for itself" attempts to be an "in itself."

One may well object to this characterization of a putatively non-constructive solution to human presence's dual concerns with terminal absence and continuance. The grounds for objection might be other than presumed unintelligibility. Consider the following line of argument: the creation of artifacts was said to involve the embodiment of human concerns in these artifacts. More specifically, human presence's absorptive drive was construed as falling under the influence of the potentialities of worldly and inner-worldly items. Simultaneously human presence's possessive drive was said to interpret functionally these potentialities. The process of functional interpretation and its result, it was further claimed, either concurrently with the execution of the process or thereafter, were embodied in the artifact. In embodying a human presence's concern, the artifact was said to manifest that presence itself. Further, once another human presence became absorbed in the artifact, the concern reemerged. This reemergence was purported to be a form of prolongation of the human presence whose concern engendered the artifact. How, if at all, does the mode of resolution of human presence's dual concerns with termination and continuance as presently under consideration—insistence— differ from this allegedly "constructive" mode of resolution? Don't they both involve an absorptive attachment to worldly and inner-worldly items and these items' subsequent appropriation?

The difference between the creator and the insister's manner of responding to human presence's conflicting concerns with termination and continuation is subtle. It may only be a difference in degree, but it is a difference nonetheless and an important one. The creator brings worldly and inner-worldly items into being. He does not, of course, create these items *ex nihilo*. Rather, he is much more the craftsman who shapes items in various ways out of preexisting materials. In so doing, however, he leaves the mark of his individual human presence on these materials in at least two senses. First, he is responsible for their organization into the particular form that they assume, and second, the nature of his existing concerns contributes significantly to the specific gestalt that these materials attain. The materials are left with the mark of their maker and are so identifiable. The insister, on the other hand, merely accumulates what already exists in finished form. He does not so much mold as collect. Because his activity is fundamentally acquisitive rather than productive, that which he comes to possess is more a set of prestructured, preshaped items than a structured and shaped set of artifacts whose structure and shape are a result of his act of appropriation. The items are his through the external relation of ownership, not through the organic relation of creative production. A Picasso painting is always Picasso's painting, even when it belongs in legal fact to some other party. The same, however, cannot be said of the possessions of the insister. The insister's mark is never left on his object except as a label. His object is, in fact, just an object, never the product of concerns. When it passes out of his legal or happenstance possession, it is no longer his, for literal possession is all the possession that the insister can claim.

In contrast to the insister, the creator is absorbed by various worldly and inner-worldly items, yet responds to them partially possessively. He molds and concerns himself with them so that out of this interaction, products are brought into being and intelligibly articulated. A delicate balance is sustained between absorption and possession. The insister merely comes into the possession of items. Acquisition totally outstrips absorption. The insister in no small way resembles Marx's paradigm capitalist.

Two additional ways in which human presence responds unconstructively to its dual concerns with termination and continuation deserve mention. One is the attempted loss of "self" through total absorption in worldly affairs. Absorption can never be total, of course. Only on a scale of degrees can it approach this state, and possessive elements are always present. Yet, there can be so high a degree of absorption that possessive elements are virtually absent. If anything but temporary, this state constitutes an abandonment of human presence's potentially creative struggle to come to terms with its basic concerns. The embodiment of human presence's concern in individualized, though intersubjectively accessible and continuable ways—human presence's manner of continuing itself beyond termination—requires the interaction of possession and absorption. To the degree that possessive elements are lacking and interaction is, therefore, minimal, the embodiment of concern is an impossibility. Make no mistake, but that the concern with continuance requires that an individual human presence's concern(s) be embodied in artifacts or events, objects movements, or situations. When this does not occur, the continuance concern is thwarted. Insofar as absorption utterly dominates the possessive/absorptive balance there is an escape from "self" and its concerns. This can be a relieving, even overwhelming experience. Mystics, participants in drug cultures, and various other human presences indicate this to be so. But if the serious business of human presence, by working both in and through its worldly engagements, is for it to come to terms with and integrate its various concerns with its most fundamental, dialectically interwoven concerns of termination and continuance, such absorption will not ultimately work. It may serve as an occasional respite, as an occasion for temporary relief from those burdens of human presence that go by the name of the human condition. But this type of absorption as a permanent life-style is deleterious to the resolution of human presence's fundamental situation.

Again, various resolutions of human presence's condition may differ ever so slightly. These differences, however, can be both subtle and important. Sometimes they serve to distinguish constructive from the nonconstructive resolutions to human presence's situation. Consider this example relevant to the discussion of excessive absorption. A human presence can identify itself with the concerns of a political or social movement. Absorption in these concerns may be the result. Perhaps no noticeable individual element is added—certainly no individual element of concern that brings about an actual modification of the larger group-concerns. Yet, this type of absorption may be viewed as constructive. Human presence acts to further a set of concerns with which it identifies itself. Though it adds no noticeably new or individualized element, its activity is nonetheless positive, for it serves to further various concerns of human presence taken in one of its plural dimensions. More or less total absorption is negative only insofar as that in which a human presence is absorbed is itself not constituted by the structure of concern. In this lies all the difference.

A final nonconstructive resolution might be termed withdrawal. This form of resolution involves the abandonment of all absorption in worldly and inner-worldly affairs and items. Neither is the attempt made to bring these affairs and items into human presence's possession. Rather, human presence turns into and in upon itself. It tries to abstract itself from those various worldly circumstances with which it is inextricably tied. Needless to say, its attempts necessarily end in failure. Human presence is concerned and worldly by its very nature. A denial of this is human presence's self-denial, an abdication of its very nature as a concerned presence. An essentially ascetic and detached resolution of the human condition, psychologically regressive in its dynamics, this attempt has no genuine hope of success.

The mode of function of human presence's extracognitive dimension in its dialectical and worldly structure ought to be clear now. Through differential eros investment, human presence is unevenly dispersed into its varying worldly and inner-worldly concerns. Some of these concerns absorb it; others it struggles to possess. Never is possessive or absorptive drive operative to the exclusion of its sometimes conflicting, sometimes complementary counterpart. Possessive/absorptive balance is present in differing ratios throughout human presence's concerns. More particularly, this presence has a strong erotic concern with the inevitable, terminal absenting of itself, together with an equally strong involvement in its own continuance. This dual engagement is conceptual as well as erotic, for the distinction between the erotic and the conceptual is but a distinction of degree, not of kind. Were no conceptual elements present, there could be no knowledge and, thus, no thematic concern at all. Human presence's fundamental concerns, however, are primarily erotic. They are more of the heart than of the mind—exceedingly difficult as this distinction is to make and hold.

Human presence's varying involvements must be integrated into an intimate and harmonious whole with its death and continuance concerns if human presence is to attain coherence and unity as a living presence manifest in a shared world. This task of integration is a preeminently human task. There exists a multiplicity of ways of responding to it, a few of which I have adumbrated. These ways of response appear in mixed form. One may be used in one place at one time, another in another place at the same or another time—each the manifestation of one and the same individual human presence. They may appear separately or jointly. To the degree that there is a pattern to their appearance, one can speak of a particular human presence's particular dynamics or, if considerable empirical data are available, one could speak of a particular human presence's particular personality structure. Throughout these methods of response the goal, which can be but a regulative ideal for concrete human presences, is the continual, contextually defined and redefined balancing of absorptive and possessive drives. Through the appropriate balancing of these drives, human presence extroverts its concerns in appropriate social, political, and artistical ways, which mentions just a few of the possible dimensions in and through which human presence makes itself felt.

The relation of cognitive activity to the manifestation and interplay of human presence's extracognitive dimensions is subtle and multidimensional. As a means of escaping its dual concern with termination and continuance, human presence sometimes throws itself into its other affairs with absorptive zeal. On the other hand, this zeal is sometimes a direct, honest response to concern of human presence with a solution to its eventual absenting of itself. In either case, or in a more typically mixed case, absorptive drive responds to worldly and inner-worldly items's potentialities. In bringing such potentialities into focus, absorptive drive enables them to be functionally interpreted in ways more adequate to their nature. Accurate cognition, construed as faithfully taking into account those items' potentialities through functional interpretation, rests in part upon the exercise of absorptive drive. This exercise may be the result of varied motives, resolute or evasive.

Cognitive activity itself is basically a dimension of possessive drive. It is an appropriate activity, but not so altogether. Possessive and absorptive drives always commingle, and, as a result, an absorptive element is always present. As indicated, this absorptive element relates to cognitive items in ways that elicit these items' potentialities. Absorptive drive, thus, is a form of faithfulness to these items' potentialities. It serves as a counterbalance to the more manipulative activity of possessive drive. Considered in abstraction, possessive drive, even in its cognitive dimension, seeks to use and abuse. In its terms, knowledge is power over the items to which it relates. The element of absorptive drive, which is present in all possessive activity, serves as a counterbalance to this tendency.

Knowledge, however, is not merely the loyal reflection of worldly and inner-worldly items' potentialities. It does, after all, involve acts of (possessive) appropriation in the form of functional interpretation. Interaction rather than faithful reflection is the model in accordance with which to understand the cognitive relation of subject and object. This possessive drive is the source of human presence's active, as opposed to passive, cognitive relation to the items it encounters. The scope and intensity of possessive drive determines in large measure which potentialities will be grasped, and how flexibly and penetratingly they will undergo transformation into functions. Possessive drive, like absorptive drive, can operate with virtually opposite motives toward the same end. The manipulative power of possessive drive, either as a means of manifesting human presence's concerns or as a means of escaping them, is a powerful force in the accumulation of knowledge.

The dialectical model for construing human presence, now explicated in terms of possessive/absorptive responses to death and continuance concerns, together with the irreducibly perspectival character of human presence, gives indication that knowledge itself is always partial, always in flux. Coming to terms with its fundamental functions, termination and continuance, is a difficult affair for human presence. Absorptive and possessive drives are prone to exceedingly subtle interplay in this process. Knowledge is both the victim and the beneficiary of this interplay, but its role is not merely passive. As human presence's cognitive activity reveals potentialities and functions, however partially and perspectually, worldly and inner-worldly circumstances are altered. This alteration is a modification of human presence's world, and that under these terms its cognitive and additional activity takes place. Such modification makes possible differing extracognitive responses, both possessive and absorptive. The cognitive and the extracognitive interact, therefore, no less than the possessive and the absorptive. Cognition is no mere tool of alien forces.

To say that knowledge itself is dialectical is to make a relatively specific claim. Revelatory of items' potentialities, absorptive drive opens human presence toward those items, worldly and inner-worldly, which stand in the relation to human presence of reciprocal presence. The more that absorptive drive holds sway, the more these potentialities are uncovered. Absorptive drive operates in accordance with mixed dynamics—partially resolute, partially evasive. Simultaneously, however, possessive drive, also operating in accordance with mixed dynamics, seeks to appropriate what absorptive drive lays open. This appropriation is not merely the assimilation of a given. Rather, it involves a manipulative activity which itself transforms worldly and inner-worldly items' potentialities into functional status in significant and cognitively fruitful ways. The dispersed, intimate, and ever-changing conflict and complementarity of absorptive and possessive drives constitute knowledge's dialectical dimension. At the foundation of this interaction between the two fundamental drives is human presence's dual concerns with what may now be termed its two fundamental functions: termination and continuance.

In my discussion and description of the extracognitive dimensions of human presence's dialectical structure, I have introduced the notions of termination and continuance as fundamental functions of this presence itself. They are, in fact, so inextricably related that it is quite likely they are one and the same function highlighted in different ways. Only human presence's concern with its terminal absenting of itself makes the concern with continuance real, plausible, and unavoidable. Be this as it may, however, I do not identify the two functions, but neither do I deny their identifiability. This must remain a question for further investigation. In bringing this chapter to its end, however, it may be well to pause to consider the plausibility of attributing to human presence an abiding concern with its terminal absenting of itself. Might not anthropological findings lend credence to the view that this is a concern peculiar to Western man—more particularly, to Western philosophical man nurtured in the tradition of German existential metaphysics? Perhaps so. The issue is open to question. Freud's investigations in *Civilization and its Discontents*, at least the Pauline dimension of the Christian tradition, and recent medical interest in the phenomenon of death suggest the contrary. But this is not a matter open to strict proof, if by proof is meant the apodeictic movement from premises held necessarily true to conclusions having the same modal status. Rather than an argumentatively drawn conclusion, the construing of human presence as inextricably involved with the undergoing of its terminal absenting of itself must be the result of phenomenological presentation.

At least five conceptually distinct but overlapping points need to be made about such a presentation. The first concerns a common attitude, having its locus in recent history, that must be dispelled. This attitude is in large measure the cause of a generally disapproving stance toward anyone having a concern with death at all beyond practical precautions such as eating well and looking in both directions before crossing the street. The attitude to be counteracted is one that envelopes death with a morbid quality. It leads to the belief that death is deep, dark, mysterious, and a fitting springboard for self-indulgent preoccupation with one's limitations. I do not wish to deny that death may harbor some legitimate philosophical and personal interest and may even be a "dark" matter, but it would be a silly case of acquiescense to mid-twentieth-century technological enthusiasm to do so. Death need not be a morbid matter. Once this is realized, some of the hostility toward any enterprise concerned with death can itself be dispelled. Clearly, there are nonmorbid, adult ways of dealing with this terminal feature of human presence. Given this, a concern with the phenomenon of death can be viewed as realistic and mature, not fanciful and sophomoric.

The second point concerns the purported fundamental character of human presence's concern with death. If this concern is fundamental, then, curiously enough, it may be quite difficult to present and articulate. It is a truth illustrated in both literature and life that human presence's most intimate concerns are often the most hidden, even from itself, and the most difficult to bring to articulate clarity. Fundamental concerns are naturally worked from, not so easily toward. Shedding light on other concerns, they themselves often remain in conceptual darkness. If fundamental, a concern with termination is likely to be overlooked. It has the character of an existential presupposition. Consider it similar to the so-called external world. So experientially uncontrovertable is the existence of this world that no argument reaches it. Many arguments move from it, however, as should be the case with something so fundamental.

The third and fourth points belong together and are, frankly, disquieting. Given the personal character of human presence's concern with death, it is likely to be the case that knowledge of this fundamental function involves the explicit undergoing of a concern with it. Rather than being open to disinterested intellectual observation, an involved, largely extracognitive mode of approach may be necessary. In this, perhaps, lies whatever force there is in the existentialist notion that subjectivity is truth. Further, if an explicit concern with death is indeed painful, resistance is likely to be met. The approach, therefore, may neither be simple nor straightforward. The disquieting feature of these two points is that taking them seriously involves the merging of philosophy and life.

Finally, the concern with death, rather than being a separately distinguishable concern in its own right, may be put in a dimension of all concerns, intimately tied to with them. If this is so, the concern with death may be quite difficult to untangle and explicate.

Having considered self-deception in this chapter, along with human presence's extracognitive dimensions as they function in its dialectical structure, I turn now to a consideration of interpretation, the fundamental cognitive mode of human presence's approach to worldly and inner-worldly items.

III

Interpretation and Its Sediments

THAT KNOWLEDGE INVOLVES INTERPRETATION IS A thesis implicit in Kant, explicit in Nietzsche, and commonplace in contemporary philosophy. Though the claim is noncontroversial, however, its nature and consequences are by no means transparent. In this chapter, through a formal phenomenology of interpretation, I shall rephrase and expand slightly the doctrine of interpretation offered in the first chapter, remark again on the process of human presence, and move to a consideration of what I shall term sediments and sedimentation.[1] In con-

---

[1] The notion of sedimentation should become clear as my inquiry progresses. I use the term "sediment" in a way not altogether foreign to Husserl's employment of the term.

nection with both the interpretation and the sedimentation discussions under consideration, I shall diagram, among other things, two alternative but complementary ways of construing human being—one inner-worldly, the other (latently) the phenomenon of human presence. In the course of these various discussions the notions of thing-in-itself, potentiality, and function will receive further consideration as well.

Strictly speaking, interpretation involves four items: (1) an interpreter; (2) an interpreting; (3) an interpreted; and (4) an item as interpreted. Schematically, the fourth is the result of the first's acting secondly on the third. To put these statements in the singular, of course, is to abstract—there is always a plurality of interpretings when interpretation takes place. More than one item is involved and the end result demonstrates that an item as interpreted is a complex affair. Even with respect to an interpreter, (1), plurality is possible. Though there may well be a transcendental and, thus, rule-guided requirement for unity in (1)—or in any of the other components for that matter—this need not preclude the existence of a plurality of items constitutive of an interpreter and unified by some interpretive process as yet unexplained and perhaps even inexplicable—given our present linguistico-conceptual abilities.

Interpreting is a rule-guided activity. Rules guide interpretings with respect to the *context* in which items are interconnected and the *manner* in which items are selected for such placement and so placed. Interpreting, in short, is a conceptual affair, and since it is guided by rules, it is normative.

The relationship of an interpreter to acts of interpreting is a highly complex matter. The necessary denial of any privileged access theory, by means of which the interpreter would simply and unproblematically be *given*, entails that the interpreter is itself[2] arrived at cognitively only through act(s) of interpreting. A privileged access theory, after all, is either inconsistent with one's general epistemological doctrine or suggests no need for interpretation at all, and, as a result, simple realism. Such realism involves the denial of significant status to acts of interpret-

---

[2] I use the neuter so as to leave analysis on a pre-personal level—not begging questions about the structures of actual personality types. Such a study as the latter is nonetheless an important phenomenological undertaking.

ing and to items *as* interpreted. Only an interpreter, now a "subject," and items simpliciter remain. This will not do. Not only does the diversity of world views discovered by the anthropologist mitigate against it, but the variety of conceptually distinct scientific frameworks does too, not to mention our everyday experience.

Acts of interpreting, to be sure, take place within a *framework*. That complex framework that structures acts of interpreting, it might be suggested, is coextensive with human presence. In this there is perhaps much truth. That a framework that *structures* is to be construed as an Aristotelian act and not as an "object" or "substance," is a thesis worth keeping in mind, if only as a provisional hypothesis. An interpreter, on the other hand—in the schema of interpretation—must be construed in a rough-and-ready way as a "substance," as that "in" which human presence finds to be its embodiment. Clearly the relationship between (1), the interpreter, and (2), an interpreting—that framework that structures acts of interpreting—must now be seen as a highly complex one, given our provisional hypothesis. It is essentially a relationship between items of two different conceptual types. Taking seriously the phenomenal fact that we find ourselves embodied, the interpreter, one might argue, is a material precondition of an interpreting. The position of one's body, the discriminatory powers of one's sense organs, and so on, do have great effect on the fabric and texture of experience. In this lies much of the truth of the "lived body" doctrine espoused by Merleau-Ponty and his followers. Certainly in some important sense (2), the interpreting, presupposes (1), the interpreter. The notion of a disembodied interpreting is untenable, if for no other reason than because of that set of problems clustering around identification and reidentification procedures. Here, also, lies the element of truth that is to be found in materialism as an account of human being.

That one finds oneself *with* a body already bound up in a world of concern indicates, however, that the dependency is not merely of (2), an interpreting, upon (1), an interpreter. To experience oneself, *qua* lived body or, more abstractly, *qua* material "object," as bound up in a world, is to experience oneself by means of a set of highly complex interpretive acts. These acts themselves depend upon the framework in terms of which they are carried out, namely, an interpreting. Thus if (1) were to be called the "material" precondition of (2), (2) is clearly the transcendental-phenomenological precondition of (1). A complex mutual presup-

position is involved. The terms denoting the *relata subsumed* under (2) are
of a different conceptual type than the terms denoting the *relata subsumed*
under (1). The element of truth in idealism is found in this: (2), an interpreting, cannot be construed in the same terms as (1), an interpreter.
Verbal substantive and adverbial constructions are necessary for (2). For
(1), on the other hand, straightforward noun constructions together with
adjectives are probably what is necessary. Of course, there may be more
truth in idealism than this linguistic point indicates on its surface. In
any case, how (1) and (2) belong together, yet maintain distinct identi-
ties, constitutes the essence of the mind/body problem. But let us return
to human presence, hypothesized as (2), an interpreting.

Human presence, (2), pre*sents* itself and finds itself *pre*sent to items
within a world$_H$. As an interpreter, I am one of the items to which my
human presence pre*sents* itself and finds itself *pre*sent. One might well
ask what is presented when human presence presents itself. The answer
to this question is disquieting. To some degree nothing is presented, for
beyond items there is nothing. Human presence, thus, not being an
item, is a nothing. But this is not speaking in helpful paradox. So little
is known about human presence, and the linguistico-conceptual framework for its articulation is so meager, that it might as well be called a
nothing. This captures the point more precisely, if less dramatically.

The functions of an item are inextricably tied to the Aristotelian act
termed human presence. For an item to have functions it must come into
and be maintained in a context of human presence, actual or potential.
Human awareness, a component of human presence, is always mediated.
Because awareness and agency presuppose each other, this holds true of
human agency, too. In both cases the instrument of mediation is the
same: one's[3] world$_H$. Because one's world$_H$ has a dialectical structure,
the items revealed in terms of it must themselves be revealed to be dialectical as well. Their functions must at once be both revealed to and
concealed from the one within whose world$_H$ they appear. This is most
strikingly the case with respect to "self"-knowledge. The functions that

---

[3]The term "one" is necessarily ambiguous in this passage. In terms of the
schema of interpretation, it can refer to (1) or (2) or to both, depending upon
one's philosophical intuitions. It is toward the unpacking of some of these intuitions that this chapter is directed.

define one as human are, as the literature of philosophy, psycho-analysis, and religion suggests, both disclosed to and hidden from one in the most intimate and intricate ways. In the case of items other than the "self"— temporarily construing the "self" as an item—this simultaneous revelation and concealment is not as pronounced, but it must be present.

The manner in which one experiences oneself determines in part the manner in which one experiences items other than oneself. From the fact that one is revealed to oneself dialectically, it follows that items other than one must be revealed dialectically also. This same point can be put in the language of human presence. That this presence is in part constituted by a world$_H$ entails that it presents itself to itself dialectically. This means that revealing and concealing are co-constitutive of all human experience, for phenomenologically human presence is the fundamental notion. From a disciplined articulation of its experience, all else follows in the realm of what is capable of phenomenological description.

To fix conceptually the doctrine that items' functions are revealed dialectically, I shall introduce the notion of a sedimented function and, along with it, the counterconcept of a nonsedimented function. These two notions will serve, in part, to connect world$_H$s with the functions they disclose. Consider first nonsedimented functions. By a nonsedimented function I understand a function as it *would be* revealed were one's world$_H$ neither dialectical in structure nor in possession of other distorting features. A nonsedimented function, so stated, is a function the revelation of which would involve no concealment of any sort. Since human world$_H$s *are* dialectical, the notion of a function from which all sediments, all distorting elements, have been purged has no readily identifiable counterpart in direct experience. Phenomenologically, it borders on being a limiting concept. In this capacity, however, it is not without value. The notion of a nonsedimented function serves as a regulative ideal in the eradication of sediments. A nonsedimented function should be construed as that full-blown set of potentialities for functional interpretation that each item possesses.

By a sedimented function I understand a function as it is actually revealed to human presence. A sedimented function, thus, is a function partially concealed and in some respect distorted. In terms of the logic of the dialectical model, however, concealment presupposes revelation. Sedimented functions are at the same time and in some obscure way revealed without their sediments to those within whose world$_H$ they appear. This revelation, left uncomprehended, is what compels the concealment and transcendentally subsequent revelation of nonsedimented functions in sedimented form. Sedimented functions are what constitute the rich fabric of direct human experience. Were all sediments to be removed, experience would in some respects be impoverished. The notion of a sedimented function, therefore, is not altogether negative in import.

There are two points of considerable importance to note concerning the distinction between sedimented and nonsedimented functions. The first concerns the relation of the two types of function to each other. Sedimented functions are not items whose existence is distinct and separate from nonsedimented functions. Rather, they are nonsedimented functions improperly construed. They are modes of nonsedimented functions, not the shadowy inhabitants of a separate realm. But this point is true when stated in the converse as well. A nonsedimented function can with equal validity be viewed as a mode of a sedimented function. The concept of a function presupposes the concepts of awareness and agency and, ultimately, the notion of human presence. Because this presence, structured in part by a $world_H$, is mediated dialectically, the concept of a function presupposes the notion of a sediment. Implied in this presupposition is the concept of a sedimented function. Consider those concepts closest to experience and at the same time transcendentally fundamental that are required for experience's most perspicuous description. Given this stipulation, the notion of a sedimented function is more basic than the notion of a function per se. The latter is extrapolated from it. From this standpoint, one can speak with equal validity of nonsedimented functions as modes of sedimented functions, modes that border on the ideal and that, from the standpoint of direct experience, are extremely difficult, perhaps even impossible, to uncover.

The ideality of nonsedimented functions, however, can be misleading. Since the concept of function requires for its ultimate coherence conceptual reference to human presence, nonsedimented functions' ideality does not place them in a Platonic realm, distinct from, yet corresponding to, the actual world of human concerns. Rather, their ideality corresponds more closely to the Kantian concept of an object of experience in his *Critique of Pure Reason*.

In important senses, sedimented and nonsedimented functions are both identical with and distinct from each other. Their identity lies in the fact that they are the same functions, their difference being the circumstance by which they are construed differently. The revelation of a nonsedimented function requires its partial concealment and, therefore, its revelation as a sedimented function. Once the dialectical mediation of one's world$_H$ is comprehended, the notion of a nonsedimented function arises again, this time explicitly. It serves as a regulative ideal for one's efforts at eradication of sediments and reconstruction of nonsedimented functions. In all phases of experience, therefore, the same functions are dealt with. How they are construed depends in part on the degree of sophistication one brings to one's concern with them.

That sedimented and nonsedimented functions are construed differently entails more than a "subjective" or psychological difference in the one who construes them. Given the phenomenological doctrine, inherited from Kant, that categoreal features of "subjective" apprehension are reflected in "objective" features of the items apprehended, it follows that sediments, the distorting or concealing features of functions, appear as aspects of those functions themselves. Not only do they so appear, but from a conceptual standpoint, they must exist as features of those functions. Thus, again, in dealing with the sedimented of two distinct items—in this case, a function on the one hand and its distorted ("subjective") apprehension on the other—one is concerned with one and the same function that is/can be considered in two different ways.

The second point deals with the status of nonsedimented functions in relation to human presence. Since the concept of presence is implied by the concept of function, a nonsedimented function does not exist in total independence of human presence. Neither is it in a conceptual sense beyond the bounds of all possible knowledge. In certain respects nonsedimented functions may be unknowable, but they are not unknowable in the same way that things-in-themselves are unknowable.

Functions, sedimented as well as nonsedimented, do have a certain independence of those who cognize them. The independence, however, is of a radically different sort than that of items simpliciter, things-in-themselves. The independence of functions is a conceptual consequent of the phenomenological doctrine of intentionality coupled with the doctrine of mediated reflexivity.[4] Strictly speaking, it is an interdependence

---

[4]This, of course, is the doctrine that all awareness of the self is mediated by awareness of items other than the self.

rather than a simple independence. Awareness is always awareness of something. It is always directed toward something which, in its human form as presence, it distinguishes from itself. Given this as a structure that is essential to awareness, awareness presupposes being aware of something other than itself. Without this there would be no awareness whatsoever. In essence, this is the phenomenological doctrine of intentionality. Its variants, of course, are many, but they all share this central core.

The doctrine of mediated reflexivity simply amplifies the conceptual commitments inherent in this doctrine and relates them directly to the concept of *self*-awareness inherent in the notion of human presence. To be aware of oneself one must be aware of something other than oneself. Since one is constituted, in part at least, by one's awareness of oneself, were there not other items of which one was aware, one would not be. That which one is aware of over and beyond the self is the function of those items. This, however, is potentially misleading. A function is nothing other than the item of which it is the function, being that item itself, construed in certain ways, all of which involve the concept of purpose and, thus, the concepts of agency, awareness, and human presence.

Functions, understood in this way, are those items of which one is aware by the process of being aware of items other than oneself. Thus, they are necessary conditions for "self"-awareness. In this capacity, they have a conceptual independence of human presence, an independence that must be construed transcendentally. Strictly speaking, it is an interdependence. Neither functions nor human presence could exist without the other. On the other hand, though items without functional status, things-in-themselves, could exist without human presence, this presence could not exist without these items. Construed functionally, they constitute the "objects" of experience. Though human presence is responsible for the interpretation of potentialities of things-in-themselves, only in rather unusual cases such as are found in some of the arts, is it the source of things-in-themselves' existence. Their potentiality-laden existence, functionally interpreted, is presupposed in the coming into being of human presence, the being which is mediately aware of itself.

That functions simpliciter, nonsedimented functions, may be unknowable is another matter. It raises an entirely different set of issues. The comparison with things-in-themselves is instructive as they are in a conceptual sense unknowable. "Ignorance" of them, thus, is utter and complete. This follows from an analysis of the concept of knowledge. Knowledge involves the application of concepts. Through their employment, items' potentialities are interpreted, thereby revealing the functional characteristics of those items. The notions of function and interpretation, thus, are essential to the concept of knowledge. A thing-in-itself, however, is by conceptual definition a totally nonfunctional item. As nonfunctional, it cannot be known and the force of "cannot" is conceptual rather than empirical. The criteria for the term's application involve appeal neither to historical fact nor to empirical generalization. All that is required is an analysis of concepts. To put the point another way, that a thing-in-itself is unknowable is not just true relative to a particular period of time or set of circumstances.

Advances in the sciences or in philosophy are irrelevant to a nonfunctional item's acognitive status. To be sure, one's inability to know such an item signifies no lack on one's part. No cognitive mechanism is missing which, if provided, would rectify the situation and add new dimensions to one's knowledge. What is involved is neither an impoverishment of nonfunctional items nor a deficiency in those unable to know them. What one's inability should indicate is simply a set of conceptual truths about knowledge and things-in-themselves, conceptual truths which, when properly understood, release one from an impossible demand.

The situation with regard to nonsedimented functions is somewhat different. Given the logic of the dialectical model it follows that any particular revelation of a nonsedimented function involves elements of concealment. At no time, thus, is a nonsedimented function known in total separation from its sediments. A nonsedimented function, however, *can* be known under certain circumstances. In this respect it differs from a thing-in-itself. Together with the sediments that conceal it, a nonsedimented function is one of the two prime "objects" of empirical knowledge. Knowledge of it is incomplete, sometimes inexact, and at all times perhaps, partially distorted.

Nonsedimented functions yet remain items of cognitive concern. Explicit knowledge of them, if it is at all possible, involves the distinction of these functions from their sediments and knowledge of both in their interrelation. The isolation of functions from their sediments, their categorization, and an analysis of their interaction with each other and with their sediments, thus, are extremely important tasks—perhaps at best regulative ideals in the pursuit of knowledge. Though these tasks can never completely be accomplished, they should and often do serve as regulative ideals in the analysis of actual experience. That knowledge of nonsedimented functions cannot be exhaustive is a conceptual truth. The dialectical model entails it. That nonsedimented functions are utterly unknowable, however, is not a conceptual truth. In fact, it is not a truth at all.

The doctrine of sedimented functions articulates, in part, the conceptual intersection of the notions of function and world$_H$. It helps to provide conceptual foundations for philosophical anthropology, a task for which it is quite indispensable. Consider in this regard some alternative ways of construing the concept of man. These ways are complementary rather than exclusive.

In experience, an important distinction is made between oneself and items other than oneself. There is more than one way of making this distinction. Consider first the following. It is in terms of human presence and, thus, one's world$_H$ that these items, oneself and items other than oneself, are distinguished. Their distinction is by no means incidental, for without it experience, conceived of as a cognitive affair, would not be possible. The distinction, therefore, is transcendental rather than empirical. Presupposed in the conceptual analysis of experience are the notions of agent and patient construed in their cognitive dimensions as "subject" and "object." The unity, continuity, and coherence of experience, its intelligibility, require that it be referred to the one whose experience it is: the "subject" of experience. This "subject" provides a fixed point of reference, a point of orientation, in relation to which experience assumes cognitive status. By "self" one might mean the "I" or "subject" of experience, the one in terms of whose world$_H$ items, including the "subject" itself, are distinguished and comprehended. I shall term self in this sense a self$_1$.

There are a number of plausible interpretations of the notion of a self$_1$. It might be construed in Kantian terms as the empirical self, an item among items, endowed with unique capacities, and studied empirically and scientifically by psychologists and others. A self$_1$, construed in this way, I shall term an empirical self$_1$. An empirical self$_1$, given the logic of the dialectical model, would be an item at once both revealed to itself and concealed from itself. The structure of its world$_H$ would make this state of affairs unavoidable. In this respect an empirical self$_1$ would differ little from the other items it knew. The notion of an empirical self$_1$, however, is rather suspect in philosophy. Hume could not find one and Heidegger does not wish to assert the existence of one either. In this they are surely wrong. Not that the concept of man reduces to the concept of an empirical self$_1$; man is not simply an item among items, the study of which is divided among the various natural sciences. But to hold that the concept of an empirical self$_1$ is in no way a constituent of the concept of man is to go too far. Consider some ordinary language statements that employ the notion of an empirical self$_1$.

He used himself as a battering ram.

Putting himself between her and the door, he blocked her escape.

He tired himself out carrying boxes from one room to another in a wheelbarrow.

Busying herself with various preparations, she had completely spent herself before her first guests arrived.

In his attempt to complete all the revisions of his book before the term began, he had utterly exhausted himself.

She was beside herself with grief.

He drank himself into oblivion.

The empirical self$_1$ is the referent of the underlined terms. Each functions reflexively, referring to the subject of the statement in which it occurs. Before analyzing these statements, however, I must reemphasize a very important point—by no means is man identical with the empirical self$_1$. My claim is simply that the concept of an empirical self$_1$ is essential to the concept of man. Without it the concept of man would be severely truncated, perhaps incoherent.

In all of the statements just listed, with the possible exception of the last two, the self is conceived as something that can be put to use. It is not just others that are able to use one; one can make use of oneself. "Making oneself useful" is an idiom that captures this notion. In the first two statements, the self is construed quite straightforwardly as entailing conceptual reference to the body. In neither statement is the body viewed merely as a property of the self. It is not understood as an entity, perspicuous reference to which is made adjectivally. Rather, the body is understood to be an essential *part* of the self. Being substantially restricted in this sense, the body is construed more like the faculty of a college than like the color of an apple. It is viewed, in short, as an indispensable dimension of the self.

With a few qualifications the body might be identified with the self. By putting one's body to use, it might be argued, one puts oneself to use, not because one's body is a property one possesses, but because one *is* one's body. In saying this, of course, one does not construe one's body merely as a physical organism. One understands it, rather, as what phenomenologists term a "lived" body, an active agent that one both is and uses. But the validity of this position, the "lived" body position, is not crucial to the argument. Without reference to the body, the concept of the self exemplified in the first two statements would be contextually incoherent. Regardless of one's view with regard to the "lived" body doctrine, in some contexts if not all, the body is construed as constitutive of the empirical self$_1$.

Not only do the first two statements make conceptual reference to the body, the third and fourth do as well. The third differs slightly from its predecessors in lending weightier support to the "lived" body doctrine. In it the body is construed less as an implement than as an agent. The body, in short, is understood more actively than passively. As an agent, the statement suggests, one makes use of one's agency in dealing with "objects" and implements, expending oneself in the process. Construed as one's body, as one's agency, one not only uses, but is. The first two statements suggest this also, but less perspicuously.

Taken out of context, the fourth statement is indeterminate in meaning. Construed straightforwardly, it resembles the third. The concept of having spent oneself, however, may have a different sense. It may refer to "emotional" expenditure. If it does, one understands the self as entailing conceptually the notion of the "psychic." Intellectual dimensions of the psychic are stressed in the fifth statement; affective dimensions in the sixth. Both are involved in the last statement.

The notion of the psychic raises numerous philosophical issues, but no commitment need be made concerning the metaphysical status of the "psyche," its conceptual locus in the mind-body controversy, or its conceptual geography in general. Whether psychic phenomena belong ultimately to the biochemist, the physiologist, or the clinical psychologist, whether they belong to all of these or to none of them, is irrelevant to the crucial point: the concept of the empirical self$_1$, exhibited in ordinary language, presupposes in some if not all its contexts, reference to the physical and the psychical. The physical and the psychical are legitimate fields of study for the various sciences. These sciences may not yield exhaustive knowledge of the empirical self$_1$, but they are clearly relevant to its investigation. Otherwise the following statements could not be true which in some circumstances they obviously are.

> Tranquilizers can help one overcome anxiety. Through their use one's world can be transformed into something much less threatening.

> Through therapy he was made over into another person. He no longer lived in a strange world from which others were excluded.

> After brain surgery he was never himself again. His world had shrunk. Things which were significant to him before seemed to have lost their meaning.

> They conditioned him to the point where he trusted no one. His world was the world of a paranoid, in fact. In very few respects was he the same person.

In these statements, worlds (world$_H$s) are understood to belong in part at least to empirical self$_1$s. Their possessors are construed as items at least partial access to which can be secured by scientific means. The successfulness of these means, even in the case of clinical psychology, requires that the concepts involved be referred in some manner to bodies, conceived of as organisms. Empirical self$_1$s are viewed as items distinguished from other items and endowed, perhaps, with unusual capacities. In particular, they are understood to be capable of supporting world$_H$s. Conceptually, reference to them presupposes reference to physical organisms possessing psychic dimensions. To speak of the meaning of empirical self$_1$s is to speak of their functions, the ways in which they make use of themselves and are made use of by others.

There are two other ways of construing the self$_1$. It might be understood as a thing-in-itself, which would be perfectly reasonable. It is also compatible with the view that the possessors of world$_H$s are empirical self$_1$s. The "subject" of experience, construed as a thing-in-itself, is merely the empirical self$_1$ stripped of its functional attributes. That such a "subject" exists follows from the nature of functions. Functions are functions of items the existence of which transcendentally precedes their functional interpretation, actual or potential. Provided that one is not misled by the conceptual truth that things-in-themselves are unknowable, it makes sense to assert their existence as "subjects" or world$_H$s.

Finally, one might conceive of the self$_1$ as a transcendental self. According to this view, the need to refer experience to "subject" in terms of whose world$_H$ items are distinguished and comprehended is primarily conceptual. The position is not without a measure of truth. Whatever the status of physical and psychical characteristics, their conceptual presupposition is the unity of the person. It is a person whose characteristics they are. One can hold this position, however, and still hold that the "subject" of experience is an empirical self$_1$. In fact, the existence of an empirical self$_1$ is presupposed by the conceptualist position. The subject of experience cannot be merely a conceptual item. Were it so, the ability to change world$_H$s, persons themselves for that matter, by various physical, particularly chemical means, would be incomprehensible. Much of the intelligible structure of experience depends upon the relation of the items experienced to the body of their experiencer. Minimally, orientation, a fundamental prerequisite of intelligibility, entails reference of items to oneself, construed as a physical "object" positioned in one way rather than another. Whatever the validity of the conceptualist position, it is incomplete as an account of the self$_1$. The self$_1$ must be construed primarily as an empirical self$_1$. Given the logic of the dialectical model, knowledge of this self can never be complete. To know it is to comprehend its functions. These may be construed as ways in which it is made use, by itself and by others.

The functions in terms of which biochemistry and related sciences understand self$_1$s are relevant as well. However these two general types of functions relate, the empirical self$_1$ presupposes conceptually the notion of a thing-in-itself, and its unity, a conceptual requirement, is a transcendental presupposition of cognitive experience. The concept of man involves reference to this empirical self$_1$ and to the various notions presupposed in its conceptual analysis.

Another element indispensable to an understanding of man I shall term the self$_2$. This notion is very close to the notion of human presence. The concept of a self$_2$ is subtly adumbrated in a number of ordinary language statements. Ordinary language exhibits this concept less perspicuously, however, than it does the concept of a self$_1$.

He found himself in his work.

They lost themselves in the affairs of the day.

He has just not been himself since she died.

When she died, a part of him died with her. This was a part of himself
he was not to recover.

She was beside herself with grief.

Self-possession is difficult to maintain under those conditions.

A man finding himself in his work finds two things: a set of items worthy of his concern and a certain integrating manner of concerning himself (self$_1$) with them. Taken together, these two factors constitute the self$_2$ at its best. Few people ever fully find themselves, however, and it's plausible to state that perhaps none do, particularly not in just one domain such as work. Less honorifically, by self$_2$ I understand the field of a man's awareness, the domain of his dialectical presence. The totality of items of one's concern, construed, ranked, and evaluated by means of this concern, together with the concern itself, enter into the conceptual definition of this field. The self$_2$, thus, is nearly coextensive conceptually with the notion of an existential world: a basic posture toward items together with those items themselves as construed in terms of this posture. From this follows an important truth: because every item one experiences is construed in terms of one's world$_H$ and falls, thus, within one's existential world, the self$_1$ must be understood as a component of the self$_2$, presupposing it conceptually and being presupposed by it. One understands oneself (self$_1$) *in terms of* one's world$_H$. In this lies the primacy of a philosophical, as opposed to a scientific, approach to man.

An integrating manner of concerning oneself (self$_1$) with items is a mode of dealing with them that enables a man to cease the search for himself (self$_2$). Ideally speaking, one ought to be able to cease this search with impunity from anxiety, boredom, or depression, chronic or spasmodic. The extent to which a man may be said to have found his self$_2$ can be measured by the degree of his integration, understood in this negative sense. Clearly, a minimal amount of integration is required for a man even to search for himself or be concerned about himself. Some integration, in short, is required for man to be man. Its concept, thus, is presupposed in the concept of man. Total integration, on the other hand, is only a liimiting concept. It cannot be attained. However, total integration is more than a negative phenomenon. In its capacity as a limiting concept, it functions regulatively to guide men in the extension of their experience. Muted perhaps, but ever present in human affairs, the goal of complete integration functions as an impetus to the expansion and modification of human $world_H$s. Not only is it important to an adequate account of the doctrines of human restlessness and homelessness urged by Augustine and the existentialists, but without recourse to it, time and human history are incomprehensible.

No less than the $self_1$, the $self_2$ is revealed unproblematically. Construed as human presence and structured in part by an existential world, the $self_2$ is known in accordance with the dictates of the dialectical model. Its revelation involves its concealment at the same time. The concealment is twofold. Items construed in terms of one's $world_H$ constitute, in part, one's existential world. Given the structure of one's $world_H$, these items, and thus a dimension of the $self_2$, are beyond the bounds of total disclosure. But one's $world_H$ itself, equally constitutive of the $self_2$, eludes exhaustive comprehension as well. Knowledge involves the mediating agency of one's $world_H$. In terms of it, entities are revealed. But by what means is one's $world_H$ itself revealed? As a background of experience, determining what gets focused as the foreground (direct "objects") of experience, it itself eludes explicit cognition. Presupposed in cognition, one's $world_H$ transcends the very condition that it imposes upon valid attempts at knowledge: the conceptual requirements entailed by the necessity of mediation.[5]

To ask the question of man is at least to concern oneself with the concepts of $self_1$ and $self_2$. Both involve one's $world_H$ and, therefore, human presence, and each arises conceptually at the intersection of the notions of $world_H$ and function, world and meaning. Knowledge of both elements, $self_1$ and $self_2$, thus, is dialectical. A determination of the precise nature of their interrelation is central to the question of man. There is another, closely related dimension of man that is of equal importance, however. Man is the being who is able to bring itself[6] into or finds itself

---

[5]Some suggest that one's moods reveal one's $world_H$. See in this connection my *Language and Being*, 140-50.

[6]However awkward sounding the prose, I revert back to the neuter here, so as to emphasize the essentially conceptual and pre-personal dimension of the foregoing analysis. "Man" must be construed now as a *Platzhalter* for the problem at hand, namely a phenomenologico-conceptual account of human being in its various dimensions, the ultimate of which, transcendentally and phenomenologically, is human presence.

in the presence of items in such a way that what it comes to say about those items can be drawn from those items themselves. Involved, at least indirectly, in the concept of man is reference to language.[7] I am now in position to specify this reference more exactly: man is, in part at least, that being that *expresses itself*, both as a self$_1$ and a self$_2$. Though not sufficient to the conceptual definition of man, the notion of expressing itself is necessary to this definition. Given the dialectical model and the notions of self$_1$ and self$_2$, a conception of expressing itself, and thus of language, can be outlined more perspicuously. This conception represents the major point of intersection of language with the notions of function and world$_H$.

To express itself is to express the self$_2$, the existential world, and thus human presence. To the extent that man's awareness of himself becomes explicit, and to some degree it must, it involves this expression. Construed broadly, language provides the means. For the first time, language fixes in a manner amenable to conceptual comprehension the sedimented functions constituting human experience. In doing this it adumbrates that world$_H$ by whose mediating agency those functions come to be revealed and concealed in sediments.

When functions are made explicit they can be dealt with. They become amenable to purposive modification. In short, they enter into the *foreground* of awareness. The distinction between foreground and background is essential to human awareness. Without it, without the notions of context and focus, experience as we understand it would be unintelligible. Language, thus, in some form or other, is indispensable to the existence of man. Only through language does there come to be such things as foregrounds and backgrounds. What language enables one to bring into the foreground of awareness constitutes the primary domain of human presence. The items in this domain, their conceptual demarcations and existential valences, enter most explicitly—though not necessarily most crucially—into the definition of human presence. The history of their rise and fall, their modification and transformation, together with the coresponding history of their linguistic expression, pro-

---

[7]See in this connection my *Language and Being*, 94ff.

vide knowledge of man's explicit and dominating image of itself—both as a self$_1$ and as a field of awareness, an existential world, and human presence itself, within whose confines the distinction between self and other receives articulation. Language, no less than meaning and world, is conceptually central to an understanding of man. In expressing man's sedimented functions and man's current world$_H$, it adumbrates man's manifest image.

IV

*Time
and Functions*

NEAR THE MOMENT OF HIS DEATH, HARRY HOTSPUR declared that thoughts are the slaves of life and life is time's fool. I find much in this to be true; or so at least I shall argue, albeit indirectly and phenomenologically. The relevance of my argument to this study depends upon the truth of the following proposition: central to a theory of human action and, therefore, human presence, is a perspicuous account of time as directly experienced by human beings. One dimension of this experience of time I shall term existential time or $time_E$. Existential time is ingredient both in the *experiencing* of time and in time as it is *experienced*. Were it not constituted in this manner, human action—human agency—would be unintelligible. I shall use $time_E$ as a means of understanding human action and of hinting further at the nature of human presence.

The ways in which time$_E$ achieves structure I shall call timings. Differences in timings are what characterize the determinants of one type of human presence from those of another.[1] In this chapter I shall discuss timings as well. Throughout these discussions, the notion of a function will be quite central—thus its inclusion in this chapter's title. Finally, I have chosen to present some notions in this chapter in intuitive fashion, rather than explicating them in detail.[2] These notions should be clear, however, either on the basis of what has been stated previously or in terms of the next and final chapter.

Consider the passage of time. Does time pass at a uniform rate of speed? If one answers this question negatively, one holds what I shall term the nonuniformity thesis regarding time. Directly interpreted, ordinary language supports this thesis. Remarks of the following sort are not uncommon.

Once the others arrived, time passed rather quickly.

In her absence, time passed very slowly.

If one holds that time's rate of speed does alter—sometime slowing down, sometime speeding up—that person holds the strong form of the nonuniformity thesis. The weak form of the thesis is that time merely seems to alter its velocity. This weak form is exhibited in ordinary language as well, though less frequently.

Time seemed to pass more quickly once the preliminaries had been completed.

---

[1]Timing, of course, is a metaphorical notion, as is the concept of an alterable structure of timing. I shall unpack these metaphors somewhat in the course of my discussion in this chapter.

[2]My excursion into contemporary philosophy of culture, needless to say, must be sketchy. I engage in it for two reasons: (1) to make the notion of human presence still more concrete; and (2) to suggest a direction which contemporary critical thought might take. Perhaps there is a third, more ulterior reason even, namely to show the *relevance* of the notion of human presence to lived experience.

Time seemed to drag after her departure.

Time seemed almost to stand still.

To the extent that time answers to the nonuniformity thesis in either its weak or its strong form, I designate it as existential time.

Whether time$_E$ is "really" a component of time is a question largely verbal in nature. Its answer depends in large measure upon which linguistic contexts are chosen as paradigms for understanding the term, "time," and its variants. The principle I follow in this regard is the principle of phenomenology and participant-oriented field anthropology; ordinary language and the experience it adumbrates must provide guidelines for answering such questions. Answers that violate these guidelines are subject to special scrutiny and require systematic justification. They are usually verbal recommendations whose character has been determined by prior metaphysical or scientific commitments. Since ordinary language and experience support the view that time$_E$ is at the very least a component of time, whatever burdens of proof, argument, or refutation exist, must fall to others—given the phenomenological principle.

Before leaving the phenomenon of nonuniformity as ingredient in existential time, I wish to note three points in passing. The first concerns velocity as such. For reasons that are not altogether clear, the acceleration of time$_E$ is a goal, I believe, that dominates most of Western culture. In this connection, one cannot but think of Santayana's definition of a fanatic—a man who redoubles his efforts, having forgotten his ends. Second, when we speak of existential times as slowing down or speeding up, we are speaking primarily from the standpoint of observers (spectators), not that of participants (agents)—imperfect as this distinction must necessarily be. Though the nonuniformity phenomenon helps to locate time$_E$, it leaves one far short of a theory of action—much less of human presence. For these latter, one must achieve a more intimate relation to existential time.

My third point is in response to those who would argue that the weak form of the nonuniformity thesis fails to establish time$_E$ as a legitimate phenomenon. This is simply not the case. Something can only *seem* to be of a certain sort, if in principle it can be of that sort. Conceptually, therefore, the language of seeming presupposes the language of being. Further, in talking about existential time, I am concerned not with a metaphysico-scientifically postulated notion, but with an experienced phenomenon. The characteristics this phenomenon "only seems" to have all work to establish the phenomenon's existence-for-direct-experience just as well as those characteristics that the phenomenon "really" has. Experience is experience. Though capable of being disliked or transformed, it makes no conceptual sense to speak of refuting, much less ignoring it.

Let us move down the participant-observer continuum toward the participant's position which is the position of the agent. From this vantage point, further elements can be brought to light including three components that enter into the constitution of time$_E$. In accordance with tradition, I designate them the past, the present, and the future. A conceptual grasp of these components is difficult. Not only do the three flow into one another, making their conceptual demarcation somewhat arbitrary, but they relate dialectically to one another as well. This flowing constitutes their unity as three co-present aspects of the same item, not three temporally distinct items. This last statement requires considerable commentary, however. In it "temporally" and "co-present" conform to a different conceptual geography than terms conceptually located in the region of time$_E$. The statement's successful explanation depends in large measure upon a perspicuous analysis of ordinary language statements such as these, together with the extralinguistic situations they adumbrate:

> He lives in the past.
>
> The past weighs heavily on her.
>
> The past had engulfed him.
>
> Having no future in the firm, he tendered his resignation.
>
> Some people live too much in the future.
>
> It is difficult to live in the present.

As a means of sorting out the meanings of past, present, and future in these statements, consider a standard way of characterizing the difference between existential philosophy and psychoanalysis with respect to their understandings of existential and chronological time. By chronological time, I understand the uniform time that is measured by and is perhaps the creature of clocks and calendars. Each school of thought takes a different component of time$_E$ as its paradigm for comprehending time$_E$ itself, the same holding true with respect to these schools' comprehension of chronological time. Whereas existential philosophers lay their stress upon the future, psychoanalysis emphasizes the past. The locus of the psychoanalytic concern is obvious. Experiences from the chronological past, real or imagined, are held to effect experience in the chronological present. The ways in which one understands others and behaves toward them, it is thought, are determined in their basic respects early in life. The various people with whom one has dealings in the chronological present often serve merely as occasions upon which fixed patterns of understanding and behavior come into play. When it is said that psychoanalysis emphasizes the past, "past" means experiences from the chronological past; but clearly much more than this is meant. These experiences, it is held, contribute greatly to the formation of one's world$_H$, *that basic posture one exhibits towards items, in terms of which the significance of these items is assessed.*

Given the doctrine of mediated reflexivity, experiences from the past enter into the constitution of experience in the chronological present. Insofar as they influence the structure of one's world$_H$, they are a chronological past living on in transmuted form in the chronological present, partially determining the manner in which the experience of chronological present is construed. The effect that experiences from the chronological past have on one's world$_H$, insofar as world$_H$'s structure has been determined by experience from the chronological past, I term the existential past as a component of existential time. The past$_E$ rather than experience from the chronological past is the prime object of psychoanalytic concern. The concept of the past$_E$ belongs conceptually to existential time and is a structural component of one's world$_H$. "Past" as a predicate applying to experiences and events, indicating that those experiences and events took place in the chronological past but are not taking place in the chronological present, is a term whose conceptual behavior excludes it from the region of existential time.

The manner in which the past$_E$ participates in the constitution of experience is dialectical. It has both a positive and a negative dimension. In failing to conform to the richness and variety of what is encountered in the chronological present, the past$_E$ is a source of distortion, a kind of distortion I have termed sedimentation.[3] Not only does the past$_E$ constrict one's ability to respond to items other than oneself, limiting one's comprehension of these items' functions as these functions are manifested in the unique circumstances of the chronological present, but past$_E$ limits one's ability to respond to oneself as well. In a twofold sense, thus, the past$_E$ limits one's ability to function.

Constituted in part by the past$_E$, one's world$_H$ is an impediment to the grasp of functions, being as it is a source of sedimentation. Those sediments whose source is the past$_E$ are functions in the chronological present, the comprehension of which is determined by this existential past. These functions are indicators of the past$_E$'s negative effects. The functions that form the intelligible structure of the chronological present are impoverished through the sedimentation that this aspect of one's world$_H$ brings about. These functions come to be viewed merely as instances of a type, losing in the process their concreteness and particularity. Precisely in this circumstance is to be found the negative dimension of the existential past.

The past$_E$ is not just a source of impoverishment. It enriches experience as well. It is in terms of one's world$_H$ that items are comprehended, and it is through its agency that these items come to whatever cognitive fruition they attain. The past$_E$ aids in this process because it is a part of one's world$_H$. Its contribution is notable in its scope and complexity. In many respects, experience is a cumulative affair. The nature of one's experience in the chronological present, how many facets of a given item or situation one is able to detect, and how perspicuously one is able to assess their cognitive significance, is determined in large measure by the effect that one's experiences from the chronological past has had on one. This effect, of course, is what is indicated by the term "past$_E$." A man experienced in a field is generally in a better position to understand the meaning and interpret the significance of various actions and events taking place in this field than is a man lacking in this experience.

---

[3]I prefer the term "sedimentation" in this context, for it lends itself to the notion that what I experience sedimently is experienced *as* sedimented or *as a sediment* (though I may not be *aware* of this circumstance). The term "distortion" can not do quite this much work. See chapter 3.

Past$_E$s have a perspectival quality to them that further complicates the assessment of their cognitive value. The qualifying clauses:

given his past experience

given the nature of his experience

and

given his background,

just to mention a few, indicate the perspectival character of past$_E$. To refer to this characteristic of past$_E$, I shall appropriate the term "background." One's background results from the particular nature of one's experiences in the chronological past. Backgrounds determine in large measure which facets of an item a person detects and the manner in which the cognitive significance of these facts is assessed. People with greatly differing backgrounds often have difficulty finding common "ground" for discussion of issues. More often than not the issues in question turn on interpretations of fact, and the facts cannot be separated from the worlds$_H$s, and thus past$_E$s, which cognitively mediate them. It need not follow that one of the disputants be right and the other wrong, however. Neither need it follow that both be wrong. Both disputants may well be correct, each uncovering a different dimension of the entity or situation in question. Though he does not tie it specifically to the background doctrine, John Wisdom suggests a view much like this.

> As we all know but won't remember, any classificatory system is a net spread on the blessed manifold of the individual and blinding us not to all but to too many of its varieties and continuities. A new system will do the same but not in just the same ways. So that in accepting *all* the systems their blinding power is broken, their revealing power becomes acceptable; the individual is restored to us, not isolated as before we used language, not in a box as when language mastered us, but in "creation's chorus."[4]

I return to the ordinary language statements with analysis was begun. Consider the three that employ the term, "past."

He lives in the past.

The past weighs heavily on her.

The past has engulfed him.

---

[4]John Wisdom, *Philosophy and Psychoanalysis* (Oxford, 1957) 119.

Though in each of these statements a chronological interpretation of "past" is possible, an existential interpretation is possible, too. It is the latter interpretation that is philosophically and anthropologically most suggestive. A man "living in the past" need not be characterized as a person whose attention is for the most part directed toward events having transpired chronologically prior to the time they capture his attention. He may be a man whose concern is focused on the chronological present, yet who deals with this present as if the same conditions that determined it determined situations whose temporal locus is in the chronological past. A similar analysis of the second statement is equally plausible. For the past to "weigh heavily on one" may be for the *effects* of the chronological past—the $past_E$—to constrict one's comprehension of and response to events and situations in the chronological present. A strict chronological interpretation of past in this statement, in fact, is conceptually implausible. It suggests that chronological time can accumulate on a person in much the same way that dust accumulates on a window sill. The best one can do in way of a chronological interpretation of "past" in this second statement is to construe the weightiness of the past as the woman's preoccupation with chronologically past events and situations. A philosophical explanation of this weightiness, this preoccupation, will drive one back to the conception of a $world_H$ and, along with it, to the conception of a $past_E$. An existential interpretation of past, thus, is at some point inevitable. A past that "engulfs one," finally, may be construed as a $past_E$ that brings about cognitive and volitional paralysis in the chronological present.

In contrast to psychoanalytic thought, existential philosophers place their emphasis on the future. On the face of it, this emphasis appears absurd. Consider first the chronological future. Clearly, events in the chronological future have no causal influence, direct or indirect, on one's behavior, knowledge, or attitudes in the chronological present. In this respect what belongs to the chronological future differs from the constituents of the chronological past. What is no longer a particular event from the chronological past, for instance, may continue to exert causal influence in the chronological present, however indirect this influence may be. The term, $past_E$, indicates an aspect of this influence. The comprehension of this aspect is crucial to a conceptually perspicuous description of experience. The situation with regard to what is yet to be but has

not yet been is totally different. Causally speaking, what neither is nor
has been is impotent. This is simply a conceptual truth concerning the
contents of the future. It implies no deficiency in what is yet to be, but
it does raise the puzzling question of what existential philosophers have
in mind in stressing the philosophical importance of the future over both
present and past. It raises still another question as well: if events in the
chronological future have no causal effect on the chronological present,
on what model is a concept of a future$_E$, an existential future, to be
understood?

What the existentialists have in mind in stressing the future is this:
the states of affairs that come into being in the chronological future are
in part determined by decisions made in the chronological present. According to the existentialist view, concentration on those events and situations that one wishes the chronological future to include, though only
those that are in one's power to bring about, ought to characterize the
focus of human interest in chronological time. The reason for the normative "ought" is primarily evangelical. Through this particular focus,
human beings can be brought to see themselves more clearly for what
they are, namely agents endowed with the ability to actively shape their
chronological futures. The contents of the chronological future, the existential philosophers stress, are in large measure indeterminate. Their
determination is in part the product of human decision and consequent
human action. By stressing the chronological future insofar as this future
can be shaped by decisions made by human beings in the chronological
present, the existentialists believe that they have brought into proper focus the volitional dimension of man. This dimension they understand to
be fundamental, for it is the locus of human freedom, the metaphysical
ultimate of Germanically based existential thought.

But there is more subtlety to the existentialist position than this account indicates. Not only can and does one's conception of the contents
of the chronological future partially determine one's actions in the
chronological present, it determines in part how one experiences this
present as well. In short, it determines to some degree the manner in
which one construes those functions constitutive of one's experience in
the present. One's conception of the contents of the chronological future,
insofar as this conception mediates one's comprehension of items experienced in the chronological present, I construe as a constitutive structure of one's world$_H$. I term this structure the existential future, the

future$_E$. Clearly the future$_E$, not the chronological future, is the primary focus of the existentialists' concern with time.

The concept of a future$_E$ is inextricably tied to the concept of purpose—to the concept of human agency and thus to the concept of human presence itself. Purpose entails conceptually the notion of chronologically future states that differ from chronologically present ones. One's conception of these chronologically future states, so the concept of purpose implies, guides one in both comprehending and manipulating items in the chronological present. The conception of a future$_E$ is presupposed by the concept of purpose. On the other hand, the conception of an existential future itself presupposes the notion of purpose, making the presupposition relation between these two notions mutual. Purposive change in chronologically present states of affairs, insofar as the idea of such change guides human knowledge and action, is part and parcel of the notion of the future$_E$ itself.

Like the past$_E$, the future$_E$'s participation in the constitution of experience is dialectical. It, too, has both a positive and a negative dimension. One's conception of the contents of the chronological future often constricts one's comprehension of items chronologically present. More particularly, one's purposes, unavoidably constitutive of this existential future, cause one to overlook or misconstrue the functions exhibited by items in the chronological present. In failing to take into full account the various functions constituting the chronological present, the existential future, thus, is a source of sedimentation. In being viewed with particular purposes in mind, chronologically present functions are seen somewhat one-dimensionally. The concepts of purpose and future$_E$, presupposing one another, presuppose this limitation. Since the concept of purpose is essential to the concept of human presence, such limitation is unavoidable.

With respect to its negative dimension, it is clear that the future$_E$ closely parallels the past$_E$. Those sediments whose source is the future$_E$ are functions in the chronological present, the comprehension of which is determined by this existential future. These functions give indication of the future$_E$'s negative effects. The functions that form the intelligible structure of the chronological present are impoverished through the sedimentation effected by this aspect of one's world$_H$. These functions come to be viewed merely as instruments in the service of particularized purposes, losing in this process their concreteness and particularity. In this circumstance, more than any other, is to be found the negative dimension of the existential future.

No more than the past$_E$ is the future$_E$ a source simply of experience's impoverishment, however. It, too, enriches experience. Through the mediating agency of one's world$_H$, items attain their cognitive fruition. Because the future$_E$ is part of one's world$_H$, it aids in this attainment. Its contribution, in fact, is quite significant both in scope and complexity. The nature of one's experience in the chronological present, how many aspects of an entity or situation one is able to reveal and how insightfully one is able to construe their functional significance, is in part determined by one's conception of what the contents of the chronological future ought (or is likely) to be—in short, by one's future$_E$. Phrases such as "myopic vision" and "unimaginative approach" give indication of the negative side of this circumstance. There is clearly a positive side as well. Change in one's future$_E$ often illustrates the positive dimension of one's existential future dramatically. Less dramatically, but no less significantly, any future$_E$ determines, in part, the positive content of one's experience in the chronological present. One's future$_E$ does add an additional perspectival quality to one's experience, introducing still another source of sedimentation. This further complicates the assessment of existential futures' cognitive value. The qualifying phrases,

> given his aims
>
> given his interest in the matter

and

> given his objective,

indicate future$_E$'s perspectival character. The parallel with the background dimension of past$_E$s is quite close. Like backgrounds, the perspectival character of existential futures determines in large measure which dimensions of an item one detects and the manner in which the significance of these dimensions is assessed. The parallel with backgrounds, in fact, is even closer than this. In arguments arising out of perspectivally differing existential futures, one disputant need not be right and the other wrong—no more so than in the case of arguments arising out of differing backgrounds. Neither need it follow that both disputants be wrong. Both may be correct, each revealing a different aspect of the item in question.

I return again to the ordinary language statements with that this analysis began. Consider the two which employ the term "future."

Having no future in the firm, he tendered his resignation.

Some people live too much in the future.

In neither of these statements is a chronological interpretation of future plausible. A man "having no future" in a business need not be a man who at no chronologically future time will find himself in the employment of the particular firm in which he "has no future." Being put in a position such as this is not entailed by his "having no future in X" as this phrase is normally used. A chronological interpretation of future in the other statement is even more implausible. In fact it is conceptually absurd. The concept of chronological time entails that one live in the chronological present. No truth is more obvious. On the other hand, existential interpretations of the function of future in both statements are quite plausible. Consider the man who "has no future" in a business. There are two basic ways of characterizing his situation, both of them existential. (1) In terms of his employer's conception of the business' development—his employer's future$_E$ with respect to the business—the man has no function(s). He serves no useful purpose, at least none commensurate with his conception of his own worth. (2) In terms of the man's own future$_E$, few if any functions within the context of the business are revealed as means of substantially realizing his future$_E$.

An analysis of future in

Some people live too much in the future.

yields slightly different results. These results, however, are no less existential in their import. A man in this situation is one whose experience of the contents of the (chronological) present is dominated too much by his existential future. He sees this present less as it is than as he hopes it to be. At its limit, this gives rise to fantasy. However, it need not and usually fails to reach this limit. Usually what happens is that the contents of the chronological present are construed in a way that relies too heavily on the future$_E$, thus unduly distorting one's grasp of their functional content. One's focus, in short, remains upon the contents of the chronological present. In interpreting them too exclusively in terms of the existential future, however, one's comprehension of these contents loses its perspicacity. This is the basic meaning of the statement under analysis.

Of the present$_E$ I have as of yet said nothing. The reason for this omission is that the present$_E$ is engendered by the past$_E$ and the future$_E$. Strictly speaking, it exists only in the interrelation of these two elements. As structural components of one's world$_H$, the past and the future, existentially conceived, enter into the constitution of one's experience. They are necessary conditions for the possibility of one's experience, therefore serving a transcendental function. In terms of one's world$_H$ items are existentially presented in their functional characteristics. I say "existentially" for items are always construed in terms of functions, and functions are only intelligible when comprehended in terms of existential time. Functions, in other words, cannot be understood by means of the rubric of chronological time.

The functions that one employs for construing items are themselves construed by means of one's future$_E$ and past$_E$. These dimensions of existential time give functions their present character and give one whatever human presence one has to them. (Here "present" and "presence" function existentially.) The notion of a function contains reference to a past$_E$ out of the context of which it is appropriated *as* the particular function which it is. The notion of a function also contains reference to a future$_E$ in the service of which it is made to function. The interrelation of past and future, existentially conceived, mediates one's cognitive confrontation with items. It gives items their existential presence to one, a presence that is mediated through functions, the dynamics of which involve conceptual recourse to the notions of past$_E$ and future$_E$ and it gives existential presence to these items, a presence of which one's world$_H$ is the unavoidable mediator. This interrelation of past$_E$ and future$_E$ constitutes the existential present.

Since knowledge is knowledge of functions, and functions can only be cognitively apprehended in an existential present, the notion of a chronological present is, from the standpoint of cognition, an abstraction. It escapes this fate only through its covert existential interpretation. This is usually accomplished by speaking of it as a "continuous" present, the conceptual analysis of which yields the existential view of time as I have presented it.

The statement,

It is difficult to live in the present.

conveys, returning to the last ordinary language statement, that a proper interrelation of $past_E$ and $future_E$ in the constitution of one's experience is hard to achieve. Surely it is. A chronological interpretation of the statement, on the other hand, is conceptually absurd. Only an existential interpretation will do.

Human action takes place *within* and *in terms of* a $world_H$. If action were a conclusion to an argument, then one's basic posture toward (and thus perception of) one's circumstances would be a major premise. Given existential time as a basic constituent of one's world, human action must be understood in large measure in terms of existential time. How does this fit, not from a detached vantage point, but from the standpoint of a participant-agent? I can but adumbrate an answer to this question, for in approaching the limiting case of the pure participant, I am forced to move away from the language of conceptually demarcated structures— $past_E$, $present_E$, and $future_E$—and to draw nearer the language of flow. By flow or, as I shall call it, "temporal or forward thrust," I mean the non-uniform speeding up and slowing down of existential time, which is both our *way* of experiencing and an *item* that we experience. Consider this first-person narrative.

> As I set about my affairs, I encounter a variety of different items. They "register" with me to the extent that they are found useful for or obstructive to my various purposes. Those items that are neither useful nor obstructive hardly "register" at all—perhaps their usefulness or obstructiveness is so minute or well meshed with my activities that "unconscious" adjustments are made of which I have no awareness at all.
>
> To the extent that an item is found to be useful, I "go out to it," so to speak, and it gets encompassed within the field of my doings and undergoings, some of which I am aware, some not.
>
> To say that I "go out to" such items is to say that the (eros charged) forward thrust of my activity, my $future_E$ conditioned by my $past_E$ so as to create my existential present, adapts them to its movement and adapts its movement to them—in the process ever so slightly altering its course. Were the temporal thrust of my activity different, these same items might be experienced as obstructive to my forward thrust. I could then either manipulate them through possessive drive so as to adapt them (the dominant mode of response in a Western technological

society, I believe), change my forward thrust through restructuring it so as to adapt *to* the "obstructive" items, or simply circumvent them. Consider now a peculiar circumstance into which I sometimes get myself. I run up against obstructive circumstances. I do not alter my forward thrust, which is structured in large measure by my future$_E$, but try, rather, to bend the circumstances to my purposes. This attempt fails, however, and I find myself unable to circumvent the circumstances either. Unable now to modify either thrust or circumstances, I find myself engaged in frenzied activity—much like a snowbound car whose driver spins its wheels at a high rate of acceleration. I find myself hyperactive and progressively disoriented as a result of the activity. The disorientation leaves me with the sense of being in a vacuum in which time flies. The "flying" of time and those activities connected with it become ends in themselves.

I shall label the pathological state I have just described *temporo-active mania*. Its acceleration, I believe, is characteristic of Western technological cultures. This follows from the fact that the cultures themselves are finally *manic*. Before pursuing this topic any further, however, I wish to present a typology for construing human action and then discuss the notion of timing as it relates to such action.

Human action may be either continuous or discrete. By continuous action, I mean action in which the "silent" adjustments of forward thrust to circumstances and circumstances to forward thrust are such that we are either not aware of them or are only marginally aware of them. I construe continuous action as ranging from the countless small adjustments I unwittingly make every time I walk down the street or drive my car to rather momentous "decisions." I put decisions in quotation marks as a means of casting aspersion on them—at least on a large number of them. More often than not, a change in the direction of our forward thrust and, thus, a change in our future$_E$, is something we discover rather than make. The reasons for such changes, however, we do not discover. It is these we invent, and upon reflection we christen the whole affair "a decision to make a change in direction." The illusion is created that the language of conscious deliberation, consideration of alternatives and their consequences, and voluntaristic choice is applicable when it is not. (Note that decisions need not involve changes in a future$_E$. They may simply involve additions to one's future$_E$ or modifications in the manner in which a future$_E$ is sustained.)

By discrete action, I mean action in which the not-always-so-silent adjustments of forward thrust to circumstances and circumstances to forward thrust are such that we are most definitely aware of them. These adjustments, too, may be either small or momentous. The more momentous ones—the difference is one of degree, not of kind—involve conscious deliberation, consideration of alternatives and their presumed consequences, and then choice and subsequent action on this basis. Usually such actions involve an abrupt change in forward thrust or in the way it is sustained. This is not always true, however. The actions may simply take the form of deliberate (deliberative) commitments to maintain the status quo with respect to direction and working out of forward thrust.

I use *discrete* and "continuous" as *termini technici*. They indicate the two ends of a continuum rather than the black and white domains of two fixed concepts. The terms "conscious" and "unconscious" would not do, for they carry certain commitments that are unfortunate. Actions that are discrete might involve elements of self-deception with regard to what is done and why it is done. To call such actions "conscious" prejudices this point. Needless to say, "discrete" and "continuous" are not altogether fortunate terms either, but when understood in the way that I have defined them, they capture the distinction I wish to make.

To complete the typology of human action based upon the explication of existential time, consider the distinction between action that modifies or reaffirms the direction of a forward thrust and action that modifies or reaffirms the manner in which the same direction is followed (or pursued). I shall term the former directional action, the latter manneristic. If I change or reaffirm my purposes—my future$_E$—that change is directional. If I merely change or reaffirm my way of attaining my future$_E$, the change is manneristic. Like discrete and continuous, directional and manneristic are *termini technici*. They indicate the two ends of another continuum. As a final point, note that directional and manneristic actions can be either discrete or continuous.

In terms of my earlier description of temporo-active mania, the dominant action(s) taking place in Western technological cultures, I believe, would have to be described as psycho-socially manneristic and, for the most part, continuous. The acceleration of forward thrust, on the other hand, tends to be discrete, though not without large elements of self-deception as regards the *why* of such acceleration.

I turn now to "timing". The following ordinary language statements will be helpful in its analysis as a philosophically and anthropologically significant concept.

He was timed (clocked) at two minutes and six-tenths of a second.

His timing was off and, thus, his work suffered.

Timing a sprinter is very difficult to do, for it involves split-second timing.

In the first statement and in its first use in the third statement, the concept of timing has its roots in the spectatorial standpoint—a standpoint that, given the travails of evolution, was probably a latecomer on the scene of history and a position of preeminent luxury. One perceives the image of a man holding a stopwatch while observing and recording the behavior of others. What gets recorded through timing is a chronologically computible duration in which certain things get accomplished or certain goals are reached. In the second statement, however, and in its second use in the third statement, the concept of timing functions differently. It conjures up a different image, for here we have positioned ourselves at the vantage point of the participant-agent. Consider again the third statement.

Timing a sprinter is very difficult to do, for it involves split-second timing.

In its second use in this statement, timing has to do with coordination of eye and hand. Involved is a kind of harmony of the senses. In the second statement, however,

His timing was off and, thus, his work suffered.

potentially more is included. Coordination of the senses may be involved, but the concept of there being a right and a wrong time is implicit also. Two alternative pathologies of timing come immediately to mind. This is not, of course, to exclude others.

(1) In terms of the forward thrust of the existential present, obstructive and useful items are anticipated and dealt with before the time is ripe. As a result of chronically premature action, the usefulness of items degenerates into their manipulability, and their obstructiveness serves as occasion for their destruction. The cause of this resides in part in the inability of the future$_E$ to encompass in a cognitively meaningful way the items it confronts—thus the vacuum-effect characteristic of nausea and

the absurd. This situation, I believe, characterizes the particular timing pathology of Western technological cultures. Possessive drive has become far too dominant.

(2) In terms of the forward thrust of the existential present, obstructive and useful items are not comprehended and dealt with "in time." As a result of chronically tardy response, the obstructiveness of items becomes, rather than a challenge, an overwhelming burden. These items' usefulness (lost because tardily recognized) becomes an occasion for melancholic remorse. Depression or melancholia, of course, serve as counterconcepts to mania and the recurrent refrain, "youth is a thing only a young man has, but only an old man knows how to use," is a fitting epitaph for this essentially remorseful form of adaptation. But there is a paradox to be found here. As the dialectical counterconcept to mania, melancholia may serve a useful function in the programed acceleration of existential time. I believe, however, that it is more typical of tradition-oriented, non-industrial societies, but this is merely conjecture.

I understand timing in general to be the manner in which existential time is structured and lived. Timing, thus, involves the manner in which time is used and the way in which the items dealt with "in time" are confronted and assessed, reacted to, and acted upon. In terms of the two pathologies of timing just mentioned, the following diagnosis might be offered. The first pathology involves a strengthening of the future$_E$ and corresponding weakening of the past$_E$. The "rootlessness" that results from this strengthening and weakening issues in accelerated activity. Always, but especially when confronted with obstacles, this accelerated activity heightens that manipulative-destructive tension inherent in forward thrust. I have termed this accelerated tension temporo-active mania.

The second pathology involves a strengthening—perhaps the word is ossification—of the past$_E$. This constricts the development of a future$_E$ capable of structuring innovatively and encouraging the temporal flow of forward thrust. These circumstances issue in the slowing down of existential time to the point where it drags—to use a contemporary metaphor. If a victim of the first pathology "never looks back" or, if he does, does so only to "burn his bridges behind him," a victim of the second pathology is haunted, I suspect, by what is purported to be an old Moslem proverb: others fear what the morrow may bring; I am afraid of what happened yesterday.[5]

More might be said along these lines, though it would be intuitive and controversial. In addition, such discussion runs the risk of obscuring the fundamental point of this chapter, with which I now conclude. Action theory, together with that account of human presence which it presupposes, is inseparable from an analysis of timing—whatever the diagnosis of a particular style of timing may be. Timing, also, is a notion inextricably related to existential time, its structural features and flow. Such as these is indispensable to a dynamics of human presence.

---

[5]This may be misquoted. I heard it in a speech given by Barbara Tuchmann and was unable to remember confidently the exact wording.

V

Towards Presence

IN THIS STUDY I HAVE ATTEMPTED BOTH TO ARTICULATE
the notion of human presence and to adumbrate its experience. The former task properly belongs to a conceptually restructured philosophy of
mind—perhaps to a new psychiatry of man. The latter task belongs to
an existentially enriched phenomenology of the spirit. In this, my con-
cluding chapter, I wish both to engage in some selective recapitulation
and to indicate something of the terrain requiring further investigation.
Using one of Wittgenstein's slogans, one might describe my aim as that
of assembling a set of reminders for a purpose. Unlike Wittgenstein,
however, I shall place these reminders within a broad historical context
and couch them in a language somewhat sympathetic to the promise, if
not performance, of phenomenological philosophy.

My first reminder concerns tradition's struggle with what has been
termed Being. For reasons that are not altogether clear even now, the
quest for Being by philosophers in the West became pursuit on the part
of a "subject" or set of "subjects" belonging to an "object," set of "objects," or property possessed by "objects." If we consider the "subjective"
side of this equation, a definite picture emerges. The subject was construed as a knower. His prime cognitive abilities required detachment
and disinterestedness for the appropriate exercise. The requisite tools of
knowledge were concepts. These tools were employed by the subject
either statically as in Descartes or dynamically and developmentally as in
Hegel. Human subjectivity was fundamentally the power to dispose ac-
curately and perspicuously by application of concepts. Concerning this
subjective force, nothing was thought mysterious except perhaps its

acognitive powers of decision and feeling. Since these were captured in poetry, literature, and eventually in psychiatry or existentialist "metaphysics," any element of mystery, if not dispelled, was greatly dissipated.

Since Kant, knowledge, the crucial subjective mechanism, has been seen to involve transcendentally the application of concepts. But whence come these concepts? Once this question was asked in a systematic manner, a further and more decisive turn was made within the realm of subjectivity. Kant himself anticipated it.

> To search in our daily cognition for the concepts, which do not rest upon particular experience, and yet occur in all cognition of experience, where they as it were constitute the mere form of connection, presupposes neither greater reflexion nor deeper insight, than to detect in a language the rules of the actual use of words generally, and thus to collect elements of a grammar. In fact both researches are very nearly related. . . .[1]

Within the domain of subjectivity, the philosophical tradition turned from the philosophy of mind to the more objective and intersubjectively accessible philosophy of language. Concepts were construed as embedded in language, and language came to be seen as the most transcendentally fit "object" of knowledge. When they were analyzed, the resulting concepts were to yield knowledge of "objects" other than language itself. In accordance with this scheme, language becomes the gateway to all the world. But what kind of a gateway is language? This is a terribly difficult question, for, among other things, it forces into consideration the objective side of the equation I have been tracing, namely, the nature of Being.

An answer requires some prior notion of the constitution both of the user of language and of that which language articulates through the concepts it harbors. These notions—human presence and Being—belong together as do that which their notions adumbrate. Not only this, these notions and corresponding phenomena, in their interdependence, are only reached through the very medium of language. The problem, thus, is circular: to comprehend language is first to comprehend human presence and Being; however, to comprehend human presence and Being is

---

[1]Immanuel Kant, *Prolegomena to Any Future Metaphysics*, tr. by Lewis White Beck (New York, 1950) 70.

first to comprehend language.

What becomes crucial to an understanding of this study is to see how this circle, created in and through the human linguistic situation, has been accepted and dealt with. What I have done is to construe the experience of human presence to itself and to items other than itself within its world$_H$ as fundamental. In attempting to extrapolate from this base, I have taken the relative balance and differential manifestation of possessive and absorptive drives as pervasive phenomena. Human presence issues forth in a variety of differing possessive/absorptive balances and with varying degrees of intensity. At its root, language expresses these balances and intensities. Language, also, expresses the degree and manner of human presence's presence to items and those items' presence to it. This dual presence, I believe, is that "ground," more basic than that which no method or discipline can reach. It is best expressed in poetic and metaphorical language. Ordinary language, a medium slightly more abstract, captures its practical dimensions; ideal languages, those of the various sciences, capture its highly abstracted contours.

That there is more of a mystery to human presence than might be thought follows directly from the intimate fusion of extracognitive with cognitive elements in human presence's structure. This presence strives not only to know, but to be absorbed and to possess. In this sense it is as much erotic as it is cognitive, highly imperfect as this distinction must necessarily be. Not only does human presence engage in interpretation that is cognitive action, it also expresses itself through the differential movement and expenditure of its forward thrust (erotic action). It is a dilemma for philosophy that human presence's dynamic development over time defies the conceptually demarcated structures of traditional philosophical anthropology. The language and vocabulary of flow is in many instances more perspicuous to human presence's description. With regard to the adumbration of human presence, thus, philosophy and poetry merge and emerge from one another. This dictum can offer little comfort for the skilled philosophical mind.

As a significantly extracognitive force, human presence is historical. It thrusts forward in a worldly way—that is to say "in terms of whichly"—and its forward thrust is, in part at least, cumulative. Its conceptual and existential worlds interpret, preserve, modify, and carry forward various "contents." These worlds make such terms' potentialities functional as well as undergo modification in the process. Throughout, the continued availability of unearthed functions is a goal as human presence strives toward greater synthesis, both of itself with items' functions and of items' functions with each other. Possessive drive struggles to bring functions together with each other and with the active life of human presence as agent. This is in large measure the meaning of technology as a contemporary movement. Absorptive drive attempts to fuse itself with functions that are themselves partially separate yet fused together as part of the interrelated structure of items' potentialities. Both drives work in unison, delicately balanced in various situations to achieve the cohension of human presence with various functions. These functions are themselves brought together by those human world$_H$s within which they come to fruition.

With respect to the dynamics of human presence's synthetic aim, a number of possibilities are opened. Driven by possessive/absorptive forces, one's world$_H$ may come to an encounter with functions that defies both its own unifying capacity as well as the unifying capacity of that human presence in whose agency it serves. In this circumstance, three options emerge. The first is for human presence to ignore and/or pass by this situation. This, however, is an abdication of human presence's reality and thus responsibility as a synthetic force, leading to its fragmentation as a dynamic possessive/absorptive agency. The path of repression and, ultimately, disintegration, is unacceptable because it is a violation of human presence's synthetic nature. It is the pathway of self-deception. Second, human presence's world$_H$ may lose its own unity as a synthesizing power. Such breakdown, however, violates the very synthetic function that a human world$_H$ serves. This alternative is fundamentally regressive and is destructive to human presence as it is construed as a vital force.

The third and only genuine option is for human presence to find a way in which to incorporate—at least to take into account—the functions that it encounters and elicits. This task may be accomplished in a variety of ways, employing possessive and absorptive drives in manners subtly intertwined. No *a priori* account can be given of the various synthetic strategies employed, for they are empirical and relative to situations. To the task of synthesis, however, human presence is driven as a dynamic power.

The notion, experience, and dynamics of human presence articulated here constitute the basis of my study, the base to which it must ultimately return if it is to succeed. I shall give further, thematic consideration to human presence shortly. First, however, I wish to issue another set of reminders that lead toward the notions and experience of human presence and Being. They concern the concept of meaning (function) adumbrated in ordinary language. As I have argued at length elsewhere,[2] meaning (functional status)[3] must be ascribed to extralinguistic as well as to linguistic items. Not only must the words with which items are described be construed as meaningful (functional), but those items themselves must be construed as functional as well. One can avoid this commitment, of course, but the price is high.

The philosophical concept of meaning must be divorced from ordinary uses of the term "meaning" and made to function solely as a metalinguistic conception. If one goes this route, the empirical thrust of philosophy is sacrificed to speculation. As an alternative to this procedure, I urge that ordinary and perhaps especially poetic language be consulted, their commitments analyzed, and that one offer perspicuous descriptions of the basic features of those worldly and inner-worldly items to which these languages ascribe meaning (functional) status. These undertakings are phenomenological. They involve on the one hand what Austin refers to as a linguistic phenomenology: the perspicuous description of the manner in which particular terms and phrases function in particular contexts. On the other hand, these undertakings involve extralinguistic phenomenology, too. Extralinguistic phenomenology is the disciplined attempt to find or forge linguistic devices to fit experiences, entities, and situations viewed as meaningful (functional) prior to their linguistic appropriation—meaningful because they are incorporated prelinguistically into a human world$_H$. Thus world$_H$ is in turn the expression and product of that most phenomenologically fundamental situation: the dynamic, synthetic movement and expression of human presence in and through simultaneously revelatory and concealing pos-

---

[2]See my *Language and Being: An Analytic Phenomenlogy* (New Haven and London, 1970) chapter 2.

[3]In this context I shall use the terms "meaning," "function," and "functional status" interchangably. As a reminder of the equivalences, I shall sometimes put one of the terms in parentheses after a use of another.

sessive/absorptive drives. It is both to and from this presence that linguistic and extra-linguistic phenomenology move.

Though not a universal philosophical panacea, an acceptance of this
basic phenomenological circumstance and of ordinary and poetic languages' commitments to extra-linguistic meaning does constitute an ef-
fective defense against covert forms of idealism. Further, I believe it leads
to the reciprocal presence to one another of human presence and what the
tradition has termed Being.[4] In this lies much of the considerable value
of the phenomenological enterprise.

Kant makes phenomenology in the twofold sense that I have indicated as both necessary and historically relevant, if not inevitable. What
secures Kant's position of preeminence can be expressed in terms of three
theses that he holds: (1) that the mediation of conceptual elements is
necessarily involved in the comprehension of the items that one encounters; (2) that any aspect of one's experience (presence), including one's
experience of (presence to) oneself, must be viewed as part of a whole of
experience (a totality of presence), as an element within a unity whose
overall structure determines one's comprehension of that unity's constitutive parts; and (3) that access to oneself is no more privileged than access to items other than oneself.

Reflection upon this last thesis leads to the view that the existence
of a world, phenomenologically construed, is necessary to one's own existence, given that human existence entails conceptual reference to such
notions as agency and awareness, consciousness and intentionality. Note
that the substitution of the term, "presence" for the terms "experience"
and "consciousness" indicates the direction in which phenomenology
must ultimately move. This last remark, however, can at present only
have the status of an aside.

Of the theses, the least difficult to comprehend is the first. It heralds
a new version of the reflective turn in philosophy. The originality of
Kant's reflective turn consists of this: he articulates a conceptual scheme
that purports both to describe the indispensable constituents of presence
(experience as presented to human beings) and to circumscribe human

---

[4]Concerning Being, see the first chapter of my *Language and Being*. There
I attempt to establish Being as constituting a respectable set of philosophical
problems.

knowledge so that such conceptual schemes are seen to be necessarily limiting with respect to the items of which they are held to yield knowledge.

Given this thesis, a number of questions become unavoidable. The first concerns the means by which conceptual schemes are isolated, brought into explicit focus, and described. Whereas some of Kant's successors, notably Fichte and Husserl, could entertain the notion of an intuitive grasp of pure concepts, for the most part the development of philosophy has been away from this methodology. The reasons for rejecting intuitionism on the conceptual level are sound. Contemporary thought in particular has effectively denied its philosophical plausibility. Language has been construed as the locus of conceptual items and, therefore, as the proper starting point for conceptual analysis. This procedural commitment presents nothing new per se for it is latent in the works of Kant and Hegel. The explicit, perhaps even obsessional, focus upon language is new however. What is important to note is that, properly understood, it can be placed in the service of a broadly conceived empiricism. Given the transcendental dimension of Kant's philosophy, an analysis of language should yield knowledge of various features of human experience . . . of human presence. It is for this reason that such analysis should be undertaken.

A second question concerns the precise relation of concepts to items as conceptual schemes introduce a limitation in the knowledge of such items. Kant's language often suggests a constructivistic account of this relation. A constructivistic account construes experience as compiled of parts. These parts are fitted together to form items that are sum totals of their constituent elements. The unity of these sum totals is provided by mental or cognitional glue. Kant's constructivism is part and parcel of his representationalist theory of knowledge. In terms of this theory, empirical intuitions are the building blocks, and the pure forms of intuition and pure concepts of the understanding are the glue.

Husserl and the phenomenological tradition react negatively to Kant's constructivistic tendencies and agree with Strawson, Wittgenstein, and a number of other neo-Kantian analysts. Because Husserl's own language has constructivistic overtones, he fails to provide a good example of the phenomenological response to Kant's patent constructivism. Later phenomenologists do, however. Whatever the activities in which human beings engage, Heidegger, Merleau-Ponty, and others argue, human beings do not construct a world of experience. Rather, human beings in some non-representational way interpret or construe the items falling within their world$_H$s. I have employed the term, interpret, and its variants to refer to this relation. Interpretation is the prime cognitive relation connecting linguistic and extralinguistic items, worldly and inner-worldly. The former interpret the latter within the comprehensive situation of human presence. Interpretation, of course, need not in every instance be linguistic, especially if linguistic involves a commitment to an explicitly written or spoken language.

But what constitutes an act as an act of interpretation? What are the structures constitutive of interpretive acts? These questions are central to an understanding of a modified, Kantian transcendental doctrine, particularly once this doctrine has been transmuted into a view concerning the relation of the linguistic to the extralinguistic within the worldly context of human presence. Additionally, these questions are basic to an understanding of intentionality itself. Once intuition and construction are ruled out as means by which one relates cognitively to the items within one's world$_H$, interpretation is the only alternative that remains. Since one's cognitive relation to the items within one's world$_H$ is a prime intentional relation, the concepts of interpretation and intentionality mutually involve, perhaps even entail one another—to deal with one is to deal with the other.

Concerning interpretation, I offer a reminder, prefaced by two valid phenomenological thesis: (1) interpretation, together with possessive/absorptive drive, are basic intentional relations; and (2) from the standpoint of philosophical methodology, the fundamental locus of intentionality is language. The reminder is this: an understanding of the various potentialities of language cannot be divorced from an explicit doctrine of interpretation. Such a doctrine must provide a perspicuous account of how something is taken *as* something—an account of how something comes to be understood to function in a certain way, how it comes to be imbued with a particular significance. In short, an account must be provided that explains the manner in which intelligibility and significance are ascribed to worldly and inner-worldly items, so as to secure their presence to human presence. The account must be neither representationalistic nor nonrepresentationally subjective. Interpretation must be construed on the model neither of construction nor of intuition.

The notion of a human world$_H$ as an "in terms of which" offers a clue to the model required. Properly extrapolated, this notion suggests five factors involved in interpretation: (1) an interpreter; (2) a medium—an "in terms of which"—guiding and at the same time circumscribing interpretation; (3) a set of items to be interpreted; (4) a series of acts of interpreting; and (5) a set of items as interpreted. Consider in this connection the linguistically based doctrine that extralinguistic meaning (functionality)—or rather, its notion—is conceptually coherent and empirically instantiated. If true, this doctrine enables the third factor to retain its extracognitive autonomy while at the same time yielding itself to human cognitive efforts. Put historically, the Kantian distinction between appearance and thing-in-itself loses its negative, epistemologically restrictive thrust. This loss, however, does not collapse the Kantian critical thesis into a variant either of subjective idealism or of common sense realism.

How this extracognitive autonomy is simultaneously both preserved and productively modified is a question whose answer is to be found at the heart of human presence's worldly presence to worldly and inner-worldly items. The answer is tied to an adequate doctrine of interpretation and intentionality, possessive and absorptive drive. Certainly Husserl thought his conception of intentionality rendered obsolete traditional realist-idealist controversies in the realm of epistemology. But intentionality is a perplexing notion. Since the "in terms of which" of interpretation is identical with a human world$_H$, interpretation and, thus, intentionality, cannot be understood outside the context provided by an exhaustive account of human world$_H$s. This leads again to the heart of human presence.

A third question that Kant's first thesis raises concerns the limiting character of conceptual schemes. Of what, precisely, does this limitation consist? In partial answer to this question I turn again to the concept of the unknowable, in the process raising some questions with regard to the notion of conceptual innovation. The problems engendered by the notion of conceptual innovation become unavoidable once doctrines of conceptual limitation are introduced.

Though not altogether consistent, Kant's own position concerning the existence of unknowable items is fairly straightforward. It is also rather instructive, both in itself and because of the reactions it engenders. These reactions are relevant to the development of the doctrine of human presence. Kant holds that unknowable items exist, basing his view on these three doctrines. (1) To explain the fact of one's experience, one must have recourse to items "outside" of oneself that "cause," or "occasion" the various operations performed by one's cognitive faculties. "Outside," "cause," and "occasion" are placed within double quotation marks to indicate their oddity from the standpoint of Kant's transcendental philosophy. Such notions, Kant holds, apply only to "objects" of knowledge. It is only through these "objects" that such terms can be used to relate, as they cannot be used to relate items cognitively apprehended to unknown (and unknowable) causes of human cognition. (2) Human faculties of cognition provide the intelligible structure of experience, doing so in accordance with rules of these faculties' own making. One experiences worldly and inner-worldly items as one does, not because of those items' own inherent structure, but because of the rules in accordance with which one's representative faculties operate. (3) If one were to take these rules seriously and construe them as applying to the causes of the fact of experience, to things-in-themselves, one would be committed to the view that items as they exist in themselves, apart from human cognitive endeavors, possess mutually incompatible characteristics. Though it makes sense to speak of our thought as contradicting itself, it makes no sense at all, Kant holds, to speak of extra-intentional items as falling into contradictory relations with themselves.

From these three doctrines Kant draws his conclusion: there are causes or occasions of cognition, things-in-themselves, that our conceptual scheme simply cannot comprehend. With the help of the following two additional doctrines, this epistemological circumstance is secured against the obvious strategy that would be employed to overcome it: conceptual innovation. These doctrines are: (1) knowledge of an item requires a direct encounter with that item; and (2) the conceptual scheme that mediates one's encounter with items cannot be modified in its actual employment—that is to say, though one can modify the scheme in thought, one cannot cognitively experience items in accordance with the scheme as so modified.

Leaving aside Hegel's highly complex appropriation of these various Kantian doctrines, the first really sustained attempt to come to grips with them is found in Husserl's phenomenology. Because essentially representationalist in orientation, Husserl's position converts Kant's theses into an argument for subjective idealism. To items, no measure of independence from human presence is granted. While denying representationalism, later phenomenologists do little more than suggest the conceptual absurdity of the notion of an unknowable. Their denial of construction as a model on the basis of which to construe cognition renders further argument unnecessary as they see it. Post-Tractarian analytic philosophy parallels the development of later phenomenology in these respects. In fact, after Husserl, the only philosopher to seriously confront Kant's doctrines, appropriate, and attempt to overcome them is Wilfred Sellars. Sellars's position rests on the denial of the last of the doctrines listed—that the conceptual scheme that mediates one's encounter with items cannot be modified in its actual employment. On this thesis Sellars is guardedly, but decidedly, negative.

Keeping this historical sketch in mind, I return to the task of issuing reminders, the first of which concerns the concept of the unknowable. The concept of knowledge involves reference to the concept of function, thus involving the notion of human presence. Conceptually, thing-in-itself signifies an item as it exists independent of human presence, but to be independent of human presence is to be without functions. In short, conceptually a thing-in-itself is a functionless item and, in being fuunctionless, it is unknowable. That it is unknowable, however, entails limitation neither in it nor in the cognitive mechanisms of its would-be knowers. That a thing-in-itself is unknowable is "merely" a conceptual truth. In this regard, empirical investigation is irrelevant and metaphysical speculation is pointless.

Things-in-themselves most certainly do exist. A function is a function of an item. The concept of a function is only intelligible if so understood. Items have an existence transcending the functions which, through human presence, they come to possess. Were one to deny this, one would be forced to accept a form of subjective idealism. The doctrine of mediated reflexivity renders such an acceptance conceptually inadmissable. That there are unknowable items is true, but when one understands what this means, the truth loses much of its force.

The next reminder concerns conceptual innovation. Once one grants the existence of a gap between extralinguistic and linguistically appropriated meaning (functions) the notion of linguistically forged conceptual innovation gains immense philosophical credibility. It no longer need be construed as an attempt to assail the unknowable. One remains within the domain of human presence, the domain of functions, at every point. Recourse to conceptual innovation becomes necessary in those

cases where the gap between extralinguistic and linguistically appropriated meaning (functions) cannot be bridged by simple extension of linguistico-conceptual devices already available. It would be impossible, of
course, to say of what precisely such gaps consist, for to be able to articulate their nature would be to have overcome them. After such a gap is
overcome, one can describe its particular nature. But the description
will be carried out within the innovative linguistico-conceptual framework, and, therefore, from the standpoint of its philosophical value, the
description will be hopelessly ex post facto.

But conceptual limitation need not consist simply within the gap
which exists between what is (meaningfully or functionally) experienced
(made present) and what can be made linguistico-conceptually explicit
on the basis of conceptual schemes already available. A gap may also exist between what can be meaningfully or functionally experienced (made
present) and that which is actually experienced as meaningful (functional). The problem here is not one of articulation, but one of world
modification.

Let us turn to Kant's other two phenomenologically oriented theses:
(1) that any aspect of one's experience (presence), including one's experiences of (presence to) oneself, must be viewed as part of a whole of experience (a totality of presence), as an element within a unity whose
overall structure determines one's comprehension of that unity's constitutive parts; and (2) that access to oneself is no more privileged than access to items other than oneself. Reflection on these two theses,
particularly on the second, suggests the existence of a world that is phenomenologically construed. This world is necessary to human existence,
because such an existence involves conceptual reference to the notions of
consciousness (presence) and intentionality, agency, and awareness.
These latter notions require a world in terms of which and within the
confines of which their functions become operational. Not only this, but
a world that is phenomenologically construed is necessary to the existence of functions themselves. Modify such a world and functions are
modified; enlarge such a world and new functions are uncovered.

Kant's own conception of a world is both truncated and abstract. It
appears in the first edition of his *Critique of Pure Reason* in his transcendental deduction. In fact, the statement of this world's existence constitutes the essence of Kant's deduction.

There is one single experience in which all perceptions are represented as in thoroughgoing and orderly connection, just as there is only one space and one time in which all modes of appearance and all relations of being or not being occur. When we speak of different experiences, we can refer only to the various perceptions, all of which, as such, belong to one and the same general experience. This thoroughgoing synthetic unity of perceptions is indeed the form of experience; it is nothing else than the synthetic unity of appearances in accordance with concepts.[5]

Kant's world is an impoverished one. We are presented with structures as might be articulated by a largely depersonalized Newtonian. Because nothing more is allowed into the basic scheme, what is left of personality is the abstract conception of an "I." This function of "I" is solely transcendental, serving as the conceptually unifying locus (subject) of experience—what I have termed *presence*. Though Kant's world is phenomenological and, as such, functions as a transcendental "in terms of which," the degree of its abstraction from human experience, from human presence as directly lived through, is immense. It is this circumstance that gives rise to the phenomenological appropriation and subsequent modification of Kant's philosophy. When Hegel writes his *Phenomenology of Spirit*, this truncated but nonetheless phenomenological conception of a world is both retained and enriched at the same time. In this enrichment lies Hegel's major contribution to the development of a truly phenomenological point of view.

Originally titled *The Science of the Experience of Consciousness*, Hegel's phenomenology represents an attempt to describe the various ways in which human beings experience worldly and inner-worldly items and the manner in which these ways are connected, how they grow out of and into one another. This very process of world transformation is construed as the self or "subject." Viewing modifications in human worlds as the result of conceptual difficulties and taking the philosophical categories of the Western tradition in their historical development as the paradigm of concepts, Hegel's own account remains quite abstract. It is not until the twentieth century that an empirically concrete and conceptually plausible notion of a human world begins to be worked out. Such a no-

---

[5]Immanuel Kant, *Critique of Pure Reason*, tr. by Norman Kemp Smith (New York, 1961) 138 (A 110).

tion is preshadowed in doctrines that are epistemologically pragmatic, and it is skeletally adumbrated in the philosophy of Heidegger. One finds it most concretely, however, in psychiatric case studies. One finds concrete descriptions of human worlds (world$_H$'s) in case studies reflecting a wide spectrum of theoretical viewpoints. Yet, these studies need not be written by phenomenologically oriented theorists.

This brings me to what is at once both a two-part reminder and a proposal for further exploration. My reminder concerns the concept of a human world (world$_H$). Consider for a final time the term, "world, " as it functions in statements such as these:

He lives in a strange world.

We live in two different worlds.

In their negotiations they remained worlds.apart.

She felt her world closing in on her.

In the sense of "world" as exhibited in these statements, one world belongs to one by being one of the characteristics that one possesses as a human being. With one's demise, one's world perishes also. Though "world" used in this sense has a number of submeanings (subfunctions) and subtly overlapping nuances of meaning (function), only two features of a person's world, so understood, are relevant here: first, that it is *in terms of* one's world (one's world$_H$) that one's experience is cognitively interpreted and, second, that entities and events, experiences and situations are found to be meaningful (functional) in the particular way they are because of the particular structure one's world (one's world$_H$) possesses.

Though reflecting common sense, these reminders represent a challenge to philosophy. To meet this challenge, philosophy must, in part, change its direction. Once philosophy and psychology were split asunder, much of the empirical content of philosophy was lost in the quest for a presuppositionless method. The retreat from "psychologism" can be documented no less in the phenomenological than in the analytic tradition. Its ramifications have been far reaching. In the case of both traditions, the price of saving the integrity of logic as an *a priori* discipline and isolating the domain of the conceptual has been, namely, the loss of direct relevance to the human situation. For philosophy to have accepted this loss was a serious mistake, and philosophy has paid dearly for it, but the price psychology has had to pay has been no less exorbitant. In psychology, the demand for conceptual clarity and the appreciation of the transcendental significance of psychological investigation have been for the most part submerged by the rigors of experimental scientific method. It is precisely these circumstances that enable Wittgenstein to say with insight that

> The confusion and barrenness of psychology is not to be explained by calling it a "young science"; its state is not comparable with that of physics, for instance, in its beginning. . . . For in psychology there are experimental methods and *conceptual confusion*.
> The existence of the experimental method makes us think we have the means of solving the problems which trouble us; though problem and method pass one another by.[6]

My proposal is that philosophy should return to the domain of psychology in a very particular way. It is not enough for philosophers to point out instances of conceptual confusion and then to clarify terms and conceptual commitments that are already present in the psychological disciplines. The efforts of philosophy must be more constructive. *Philosophers must articulate the structures of that mediated reflexivity that both is man as well as the context within which man emerges as an object for empirical investigation.* Methodologically, phenomenology provides the means for this articulation. But the full accomplishment of the task will not be easy. The burden of phenomenology is especially multi-dimensional when it comes to a constructive articulation of subject matters traditionally classified as psychological. One of phenomenology's first tasks, in fact, is to enlarge this traditional system of classification so that psychiatry and law come to be seen as central to psychology and thus to a concretely transcendental phenomenology of man.

The purpose of a phenomenological investigation of psychiatry is the conceptual clarification of the structures of human worlds (world$_H$s). Most often and most painstakingly observed and recorded by psychiatrists, it is during these periods of severe and enduring stress that the dynamics of human worlds become most evident. Such periods are referred to by the existentialist tradition as periods in which individuals

---

[6]Ludwig Wittgenstein, *Philosophical Investigations*, tr. by G. E. M. Anscombe (New York, 1958) 232e.

are confronted quite explicitly with boundary situations—situations that they can neither escape nor control. I shall not argue the relative merits of distinguishing between existential and psychopathological forms of anxiety. What I want to urge is simply this: the context of psychiatry provides an especially valuable experiential base for the conceptual illumination of mediated reflexivity in its diverse structures. In other words, the psychiatric situation offers an empirical avenue of approach to the conceptual problems involved in understanding man. Phenomenologically, one must be less concerned with what is said *about* patients than with what patients themselves say and do and how they *view* items—in short, with their behavior, verbal and nonverbal, and their world$_H$s.

This material is recorded in psychiatric case studies. To distinguish what, in a broad sense, is given when viewed in terms of a particular psychiatric theory is by no means an easy task, but it is not an impossible one. Clearly, it is an element of philosophy to achieve a perspicuous separation of these elements, as perspicuous as the inexact but unavoidable "sciences" of philosophy will allow. What one strives to attain in every case is an empirically grounded articulation of the dynamics of human worlds. The progress of philosophy toward the achievement of this end has, at best, been uneven. Moreover, progress in this area is quite difficult to assess. Philosophy has moved from the abstract mechanism of Kant's transcendental doctrines though Hegel's conceptually motivated, dialectically developed phenomenology of spirit, Kierkegaard's truncated dialectic of the "unhappy consciousness," and Nietzsche's aphoristic insights into the aggressive, self-affirming instincts at the root of world views, to twentieth-century phenomenological psychiatry. As its most influential proponents, Boss and Binswanger, explain it, phenomenological psychiatry is finally the application of Heideggerian insights to the domain of psychotherapy.[7] These insights, however, clearly are derived from Nietzsche and perhaps even more particularly from Kierkegaard.

---

[7]In this connection see Ludwig Binswanger, *Being-in-the World: Selected Papers of Ludwig Binswanger*, tr. by Jacob Needleman (New York, 1968). See especially 206ff. See also Medard Boss, *Psychoanalysis and Daseinsanalysis*, tr. by Ludwig Lefebre (New York, 1963).

It would be no exaggeration to say that in the twentieth century the task of understanding man has for the most part fallen to psychiatry, being pragmatically oriented in England and America, existentially oriented on the continent. Both schools bear the marks of Freudian thought. A return of philosophy to its traditional role as the guardian of the image of man must come through philosophers concerning themselves with the phenomenon of man, psychiatrically revealed. If philosophy is to be both comprehensive and relevant to the human situation, it has no choice but to follow this course. Finally, a phenomenological approach to the subject matter of psychiatry need not entail Heideggerian solutions to philosophically anthropological problems. Whether it does, only time—which an empirically grounded approach requires—can determine. Certainly philosophy, whether conceived as a phenomenological or nonphenomenological discipline, cannot do without the conception of a human world. Much is left open, however, with regard to what this entails.

When properly analyzed, law no less than psychiatry yields important insights in the service of a phenomenologically articulated psychology. This moves from the centrality of the concept of function to an understanding of man—man cannot be understood apart from the concepts of agency and awareness. Neither agency nor awareness are intelligible without recourse to the concept of function. It is at this point that the philosophical significance of law emerges. The law must constantly deal with *marginal* situations. A marginal situation is a situation in which conceptual, quasidefinitional questions concerning the uses (functions) to which men put themselves and to which they are put by other men are central. It is these questions that constitute these situations' marginal character, making such situations not only legally but philosophically significant. An analysis of the language of the law, together with perspicuous descriptions of the situations that this language reflects, cannot but be phenomenologically significant. To be quite specific, marginal situations provide an empirically grounded base for conceptual clarification of the multidimensional, normatively charged notion of function.

From the task of providing historical pointers and issuing reminders, I return to human presence. I have construed this presence as a worldly and synthetic force, motivated by possessive and absorptive drive, and cognitively revelatory and concealing. Language is its most significant and most fundamental possession as well as, paradoxically, its master; and self-deception is the cancer at the heart of human presence. This, I believe, constitutes the basic gestalt in accordance with which to construe human presence and, thus, man. As a philosophically dialectical notion, human presence undoubtedly raises as many problems as it solves. This, however, is as it should be and indicates no lack of progress. The interplay of light and darkness, conceptual perspicuity and opacity, is central to human nature and its most luminously mysterious product—the philosophical enterprise. It is to the continuance of this enterprise that the present study is directed.

Index